Warfare in the Modern World

HISTORY OF WARFARE

R.G. Grant

RSVP

RAINTREE STECK-VAUGHN
PUBLISHERS
A Steck-Vaughn Company

Austin, Texas

www.steck-vaughn.com

Steck-Vaughn Company

First published 1999 by Raintree Steck-Vaughn Publishers,
an imprint of Steck-Vaughn Company.
Copyright © 1999 Brown Partworks Limited.

Library of Congress Cataloging-in-Publication Data

Grant, R. G.
   Warfare in the modern world, 1945–2000 / R. G. Grant.
      p.   cm. — (History of warfare)
   Includes bibliographical references and index.
   ISBN 0-8172-5452-8
      1. Military history, Modern--20th century.   2. Military art and
science--History--20th century.   I. Title.   II. Series: History of
warfare (Austin, Tex.)
   U42.G73   1999
   355'.009'04--dc21
                                                      98-31451
                                                      CIP

Printed and bound in the United States
1 2 3 4 5 6 7 8 9 0 IP 03 02 01 00 99 98

Brown Partworks Limited
Managing Editor: Ian Westwell
Senior Designer: Paul Griffin
Picture Researcher: Wendy Verren
Editorial Assistant: Antony Shaw
Cartographer: William le Bihan
Index: Pat Coward

Raintree Steck-Vaughn
Publishing Director: Walter Kossmann
Project Manager: Joyce Spicer
Editor: Shirley Shalit

Front cover: U.S. troops establish a firebase in South Vietnam in the 1960s (main picture) and UN peace-keeping forces in Bosnia, 1990s (inset).
Page 1: Portuguese troops on patrol in their colony of Angola, West Africa, in the 1970s.

Consultants
Professor Ken Hamburger,
American Military University,
Manassas, Virginia
Dr. Niall Barr, Senior Lecturer,
Royal Military Academy Sandhurst,
Camberley, Surrey, England

Acknowledgments listed on page 80 constitute part of this copyright page.

CONTENTS

INTRODUCTION

The end of World War II in 1945 did not herald the beginning of an age of peace. The various Allies who had beaten Germany and Japan soon split along political lines. One group was dominated by the United States; the other by the Soviet Union. Europe was also split in two.

After 1945 the United States and the Soviet Union started an undeclared conflict, known as the Cold War, which lasted until the 1980s. Both sides built up the strength of their armed forces and enlarged their arsenals of nuclear weapons. The two superpowers never actually went to war, but involved themselves in supporting regimes that opposed their rival, spying, and protecting those countries and areas of the globe they considered to be within their own spheres of influence.

Although the United States and the Soviet Union did not go to war, most of the world has, at one time or another, seen fighting since 1945. The two superpowers have themselves been involved in large-scale wars, most notably the U.S. in Vietnam (1965–75) and the Soviet Union in Afghanistan (1979–88).

Other wars have involved regional powers attacking their neighbor to capture disputed territory. Nationalist guerrillas, groups that avoid large battles but use ambushes and hit-and-run raids, have campaigned to gain their independence from European colonial powers. Since 1945 the world has also seen the growth of terrorism, which has forced many nations to form antiterrorist units.

Nuclear weapons have not been used in anger since 1945, but modern conventional, non-nuclear, weapons have nevertheless taken a heavy toll of human life. Estimates suggest that about 50 million civilians have died in wars since World War II and a much larger number have suffered from the impact of conflicts.

Warfare since 1945 has been dominated by rapid advances in military technology. Weapons of all types have become more powerful, flexible, and capable of inflicting huge casualties. Aircraft, for example, can fly farther, faster, carry a greater variety of weapons, and hit a target with greater accuracy than ever before. However, modern equipment is hugely expensive and prone to mechanical failure. Few countries can finance fully-modern armed forces and those that do spend great sums keeping their weapons in serviceable order.

There can be little doubt that warfare will not disappear. History shows that countries are always ready to use violence to either defend or extend their influence and power. The United Nations, the international body dedicated to resolving conflicts, has had some successes in limiting wars, but it cannot stop them from breaking out if those involved are determined to use force to settle their differences.

For some countries the world has become a less dangerous place since the end of the Cold War in the late 1980s, but for others the threat of conflict is an ever-present danger.

REVOLUTION IN CHINA

In 1911 a revolution overthrew the long-standing Manchu dynasty in China and the country became a republic. However, the revolution failed to provide China with the strong government that it needed to end years of political unrest. Most of China was controlled by warlords, powerful military leaders who ruled as dictators in their own areas. In 1926 the main political party in the Chinese Republic, the Kuomintang, launched a military campaign against the warlords. This campaign began over 20 years of warfare in China.

The Kuomintang armies were commanded by General Chiang Kai-shek. They had the support of the Chinese Communist party, which had been founded in 1921 and had allied itself with the Kuomintang. Chiang Kai-shek's campaign was highly successful. By 1927 he had gained control of most of China. Feeling in a strong position, he then turned against his Communist allies, whom he mistrusted. He banned the Communist party and killed many thousands of Communists, as well as crushing uprisings in cities such as Canton and Shanghai.

Kuomintang troops stand guard at the gates to a Chinese city during their campaign against Chinese warlords in the late 1920s.

Those Communists who survived Chiang Kai-shek's harsh measures fled to the countryside. In 1928 Chiang Kai-shek set up a Nationalist government in Nanking, which became the Chinese capital until 1949, and he was soon widely recognized as the country's legitimate ruler. The Communists continued to resist him, however, and set up their own government in Jiangxi province in 1931.

Winning over the peasants

Mao Zhedong, the son of a peasant farmer, became the head of the Chinese Communists. Traditionally, Marxism had taught that city-based factory workers would be the spearhead of revolution. But Mao argued that Chinese peasants could provide the basis for a revolution achieved through waging war in the countryside. Marxism, out of which Communism grew, was developed by a German philosopher,

Karl Marx, in the 19th century. Marx believed that the urban working class would have to resort to political violence to destroy the ruling elite before they could achieve power.

At first, however, it seemed the Communists might be wiped out in China. They were forced to flee from Jiangxi to escape extermination by Chiang Kai-shek's forces in 1934. After the hardships of the Long March, as the Communists' escape from Jiangxi became known, they reached the remote Shaanxi province in 1935. There they began to build up support among the peasants and prepared to attack the Kuomintang.

The support of the peasants was the key to the Communists' eventual victory. Whereas the Kuomintang (also known as the Nationalists) stole food from the peasants, the Communists usually paid. The Communists also freed peasants from the burden of debts and high rents by banishing or killing local officials who had collected money from the peasants. The Kuomintang was

China was torn apart by war for most of the first half of the 20th century. Part of the conflict was between Chinese Nationalist forces led by Chiang Kai-shek and Communist forces led by Mao Zhedong. Mao came close to defeat in 1934–35, but his troops escaped due to the Long March. This escape paved the way for Mao's final victory over Chiang in 1949.

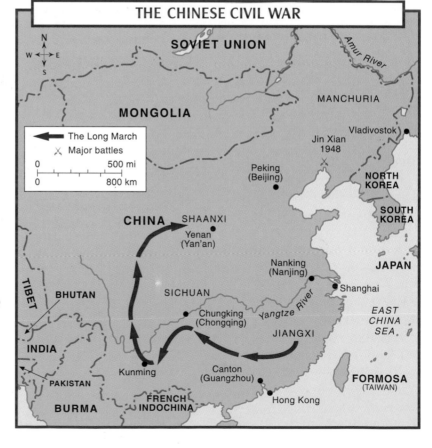

THE CHINESE CIVIL WAR

← The Long March
✕ Major battles

0   500 mi
0   800 km

SOVIET UNION

MONGOLIA

MANCHURIA

Vladivostok

Jin Xian
1948

Peking
(Beijing)

NORTH
KOREA

SOUTH
KOREA

CHINA   SHAANXI
Yenan
(Yan'an)

Nanking
(Nanjing)

JAPAN

Shanghai

TIBET   BHUTAN   SICHUAN

Chungking
(Chongqing)   Yangtze River

EAST
CHINA
SEA

JIANGXI

INDIA

Kunming

Canton
(Guangzhou)

FORMOSA
(TAIWAN)

PAKISTAN

FRENCH
INDOCHINA   Hong Kong

BURMA

THE LONG MARCH

In October 1934, Chinese Communist forces broke out of Jiangxi province in southern China, where they had been encircled by the Kuomintang. Their aim was to establish a new base where they could be reasonably secure from Kuomintang attacks.

Traveling between 40 and 60 miles (64–96 km) a day, about 120,000 Communists headed west into Sichuan, and then north toward remote Shaanxi province. The journey was hazardous, crossing an almost impassable terrain of deserts and mountains, cut by deep gorges. The Communists were harassed by Kuomintang troops, as well as by local bandits and warlords, along the route. Thousands died of cold and hunger.

The Long March took a year to complete. Only 20,000 Communists finally made it to Shaanxi. But they were enough to provide the core from which a reborn Chinese Communist movement could grow. The Long March also established Mao Zhedong as the unquestioned leader of the Chinese Communist party.

Chinese Communist forces move through harsh terrain during the Long March.

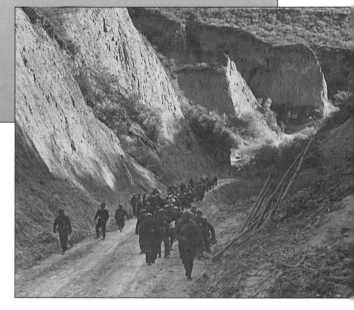

identified with the landlords, who were hated by the peasants. Mao troops killed landlords and other "oppressors."

In 1937 the Japanese invaded China, where they wanted to carve out an empire. Mao and Chiang Kai-shek declared a truce in their war to resist the invader, creating the Anti-Japanese United Front. Despite this alliance, Japanese forces soon occupied most of northern and eastern China. Although fighting occasionally flared up between the Nationalists and Communists, the truce in their struggle basically held until 1945, when the Japanese were thrown out of China.

The Communists fought a guerrilla war of hit-and-run raids and ambushes against the Japanese in occupied areas of rural China. This allowed them to spread their influence over wider areas of the countryside. It also made many Chinese feel that the Communists were the true champions of Chinese independence.

MAO ZHEDONG'S REVOLUTIONARY WARFARE

Between 1927 and 1949, Mao Zhedong developed a theory of "people's war," based on his experience of the fighting in China and on his reading of ancient Chinese military writers.

He believed that a revolutionary war had to start in the countryside. His Communist forces survived among the peasants, as Mao said, "like fish in the sea." Although militarily weaker than their enemies, the revolutionaries had a stronger will to fight. They never stood their ground against superior enemy forces, only giving battle when they had a local advantage in numbers and weapons that gave them a good chance of victory.

The aim of Mao's type of warfare was to weaken and demoralize the enemy. With time on their side the revolutionaries waited for their enemies to begin to collapse. Then, when the time was right, they came into the open, launching a conventional military offensive to take over the cities and win power.

Chiang, however, was widely blamed for failing to prevent the Japanese occupation. In 1945, after the defeat of Japan at the end of World War II (during which China was an important ally of the U.S. and Britain), the war between the Nationalists and the Communists soon broke out again.

On paper the Nationalists still had stronger forces. They also enjoyed the support of the most powerful country in the world, the United States. But the Kuomintang leadership had become corrupt and unpopular, and the rank and file suffered from poor morale. Desertion was a major problem for Kuomintang armies. In contrast, the Communists were able to recruit hundreds of thousands of fresh troops from the peasantry.

Communist victory

The Soviet Union, which had occupied the Chinese province of Manchuria at the end of World War II, allowed Mao's forces to establish themselves there in 1945–46. Chiang Kai-shek ill-advisedly launched an offensive to retake Manchuria. His troops were able to occupy the Manchurian cities, but were then encircled by rural-based Communist forces. The Nationalists suffered a string of defeats. The Communist forces, known since 1946 as the People's Liberation Army (PLA), were soon strengthened with large quantities of captured equipment and deserting Nationalist troops, who enrolled in the PLA in their tens of thousands.

By 1948 the PLA was in full control of Manchuria. The Communist forces then pushed southward. They inflicted a catastrophic defeat on Chiang's armies in a battle around Jin Xian in October, in which about 500,000 Nationalist troops were either killed, wounded, or taken prisoner. By this time, the economies in Nationalist areas were collapsing. Soldiers' pay was worthless, removing the only reason for fighting. The Kuomintang armies began to fall apart. Hundreds of thousands of troops deserted to the Communist side, where they were better treated and seemed to be moving with the tide of victory.

Recognizing Communist China

In April 1949, the PLA crossed the Yangtze River and began to occupy southern China. By the last months of the year almost all of mainland China was under Communist control. In October 1949, in Beijing, the new capital, Mao Zhedong proclaimed the People's Republic of China. Chiang and his followers, who had fled to the island of Formosa, now Taiwan, continued to claim to be the legitimate Chinese government. They remained safe from Communist assault because of the protection offered by the United States, which until 1972 recognized the Nationalist leadership in Taiwan as the legitimate government of all China.

A crowd of over 300,000 gathers in central Beijing on October 1, 1949, to hear Mao Zhedong proclaim the creation of the Communist People's Republic of China. A large portrait of Mao hangs from the wall.

WAR IN INDOCHINA

Fance's Indochina colony, created in the second half of the 19th century, consisted of Tonkin, Annam, and Cochin China—collectively known as Vietnam—and Laos and Cambodia. In 1930 Ho Chi Minh, a revolutionary, founded the Indochinese Communist party, which was dedicated to liberating Indochina. The Communists had little influence in Indochina until the defeat of France by Germany in 1940 at the beginning of World War II, which was followed by the occupation of Indochina by Japan, Germany's ally. Vietnam was plunged into the first of a series of wars of national liberation.

In 1941 the anti-French Vietnamese created a nationalist movement in the northernmost part of Vietnam, Tonkin. Normally known as the Viet Minh, this Communist-dominated movement, also attracted support from other groups hostile to the French and Japanese. Ho's leading military deputy, Vo Nguyen Giap, began a guerrilla campaign of hit-and-run raids and ambushes to throw out the Japanese and, after World War II, the French.

At first the Viet Minh was a small organization with almost no military power. Operations against the Japanese did not start in earnest until 1944. However, the Viet Minh was well placed to take advantage of the confused events of early 1945. First, the French forces that had continued to keep order in Indochina during the Japanese occupation were suddenly imprisoned or confined to a particular area by the Japanese. This allowed the Viet Minh to extend their influence. Then Japanese power collapsed with their surrender of August 1945 at the end of World War II.

Vo Nguyen Giap, the head of the Viet Minh's military wing (left), lectures a group of recruits during the party's campaign to throw the Japanese out of Indochina in World War II.

Immediately after the Japanese surrender, Ho Chi Minh occupied the city of Hanoi in the north and declared himself president of an independent Democratic Republic of Vietnam with Hanoi as its capital. In the south, where the Viet Minh was weaker and the British moved troops in to supervise the Japanese surrender, French colonial power was restored. In the north, however, the Viet Minh remained in control. On March 6, 1946, France formally recognized the Democratic Republic of Vietnam as a self-governing part of the French empire. Lulled by this compromise, Ho allowed French forces to enter Hanoi and Haiphong, the chief port.

A campaign of terror

In November 1946, clashes between Ho's supporters and the French increased in Haiphong. The city was bombarded by the French fleet, and 6,000 people died. The following month, the Viet Minh withdrew from Hanoi to the north's isolated interior and resumed the guerrilla war. The French garrisoned many northern cities and towns. The Viet Minh, now stronger and better armed than before, harassed the French with ambushes and skirmishes. The guerrillas slowly extended their hold over much of the rural north, terrorizing village elders and killing government officers who remained loyal to the French. These attacks marked the start of the French–Indochina War, which lasted until 1954.

Neighboring China fell to the Communists in 1949 (see pages 5–9). This opened up supply routes and safe havens for the Viet Minh in China. French outposts near the Chinese border were now vulnerable to attack. During 1950 a fierce battle was fought over a key highway, the only link between Hanoi and Cao Bang, a vital town near the Chinese border. Eventually the Viet Minh won the struggle for Dong Khe, the key to the route, and a great number of Cao Bang's French garrison were killed.

VO NGUYEN GIAP

Vo Nguyen Giap was one of the most successful military leaders of the 20th century. A history teacher before he joined the Indochinese Communist party in 1930, Giap was appointed military commander of the Viet Minh in 1941. Out of nothing, he built up a guerrilla army that was eventually capable of taking on and beating the French colonial forces.

In the 1960s and 1970s, as the defense minister of North Vietnam, he masterminded the defeat of American forces in the Vietnam War and the eventual conquest of South Vietnam (see pages 58–67).

Giap's leadership was characterized by iron determination and superb organizational ability. He made mistakes, such as the frontal attack on the Red River delta in 1951, and his tactics were often wasteful of lives. But he never lost sight of the political and psychological elements in warfare, seeking victory in the minds of his enemies as much as on the battlefield.

The Viet Minh's war against the French in Indochina lasted from 1946 until 1954. The Viet Minh tended to avoid fighting major French forces, preferring to attack isolated garrisons or launch ambushes. However, during the war's decisive battle at Dien Bien Phu in 1953–54 the Viet Minh did take on the French directly. The French surrendered and Indochina was split into two counties, North and South Vietnam. The Viet Minh remained committed to uniting the two countries.

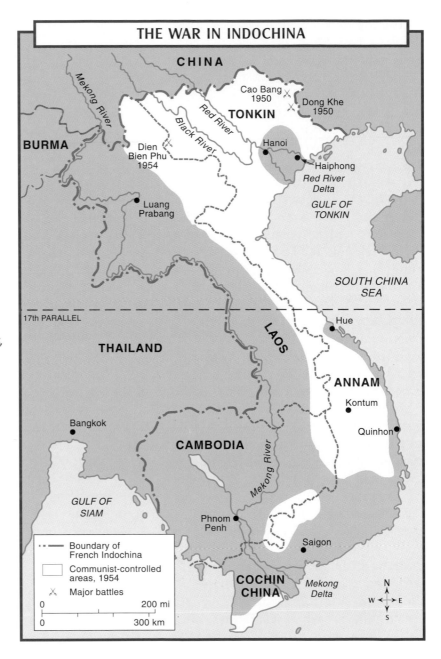

THE WAR IN INDOCHINA

Emboldened by this success, in 1951 Giap decided to launch an offensive to seize the vital Red River delta and possibly end the war. But the French were now commanded by General Jean de Lattre de Tassigny, who had built fortifications to defend the delta. The Viet Minh assaults were beaten off.

Giap recovered swiftly from his mistake. He reverted to guerrilla tactics, to which the French had no answer. The roads on which those French forces defending key towns and villages largely depended for supply and reinforcement were hopelessly vulnerable to ambush and sabotage. Nor could the French prevent terrorist attacks in urban areas, which undermined morale.

The decisive battle

In May 1953, General Henri Navarre was put in charge of saving the French position. Giap's forces may have numbered 200,000 at this time. Navarre gambled on a decisive battle at Dien Bien Phu, some 200 miles (320 km) west of Hanoi. French troops, the first of 15,000, parachuted into Dien Bien Phu in November 1953.

The base Navarre constructed at Dien Bien Phu was intended as a lure. It was to be the killing field on which he would destroy the Viet Minh. Giap eagerly took up the challenge. He assembled a powerful force that laid siege to the base in March 1954. In vain, the French appealed to the United States to use its airpower—even the atom bomb—to prevent a Viet Minh victory. The U.S. government refused, and Dien Bien Phu was overrun on May 7.

The defeat at Dien Bien Phu was a shock to the French. The French agreed to independence for Laos, Cambodia, and Vietnam. However, Vietnam was temporarily divided in two at the 17th Parallel pending nationwide elections. The elections were never held. North Vietnam became a Communist state under Ho Chi Minh, and South Vietnam was run by the U.S.-backed regime of Vietnamese politician Ngo Dinh Diem. The seeds of the later Vietnam War were sown.

DIEN BIEN PHU

The key to the Viet Minh victory at Dien Bien Phu was supply. In almost impassable terrain, General Giap assembled and supplied an army of about 40,000 men around the French base, complete with heavy artillery supplied by the pro-Viet Minh Chinese government. The airstrip at the base, on which the French depended for resupply, was smashed by shelling almost as soon as the Viet Minh onslaught began. Although the French parachuted in some supplies and reinforcements, they were inadequate.

The Viet Minh's artillery was positioned on the reverse (rear) slopes of the hills that ringed the base. Out of range of French artillery, the guns bombarded the besieged troops. Giap could have waited for the inevitable French surrender, but the Viet Minh were ordered to carry out mass assaults until the French defenses were overrun.

A helicopter brings in supplies to the French garrison of Dien Bien Phu.

THE FIGHT FOR KOREA

After the defeat of Japan at the end of World War II, Korea was divided between a Soviet Union-occupied zone in the north and an American zone in the south. The Soviet zone of occupation became the Communist Democratic People's Republic of Korea—North Korea—ruled by Kim Il Sung, and the American zone became the Republic of Korea—South Korea—ruled by Syngman Rhee. However, each of the Korean regimes claimed to be the government of the whole country. North Korea planned to invade the South.

From 1949 tension between North and South Korea grew and there were frequent clashes between their forces along the 38th Parallel, the line of the border between the two states. On June 25, 1950, Kim Il Sung launched a massive invasion of the South. Committed to resisting the spread of Communism around the globe, the United States wanted to intervene militarily in defense of South Korea. The Americans called on the United Nations to authorize armed intervention. By chance, the Soviet representative to the UN, who could have voted against any UN action, had

U.S. Marines storm ashore at Inchon, South Korea, on September 15, 1950. The landings behind the North Korean front line were a great success and forced the North Koreans to retreat.

temporarily withdrawn from the organization in protest over another matter. So the UN ordered a force to South Korea.

Although many other countries, including Britain, France, Canada, Australia, and New Zealand, aided the UN effort, about 300,000 out of the 345,000-strong UN force that fought in Korea were from the United States. The UN forces were placed under General Douglas MacArthur with orders to re-unify the peninsula.

Attack and counterattack

The initial 1950 North Korean onslaught swept through the South Korean defenses. The South Korean capital, Seoul, fell into Communist hands. Both South Korean and American troops were forced back into a position around the port of Pusan in the south, defending an area that became known as the Pusan Perimeter. However, MacArthur counterattacked with a bold amphibious (by land and sea) landing at Inchon, a port behind the North Korean front line to the west of Seoul, on September 15. By the end of the month UN forces had recaptured Seoul and the North Koreans were in full retreat.

The Communist government of China gave clear warning that it would intervene in the conflict if the UN forces invaded North Korea. But MacArthur had no intention of halting his advance north from Seoul at the North Korean border. He told the U.S. government: "Unless and until the enemy capitulates, I regard all of Korea open to our military operations." By the last week in October, UN forces had advanced northward to within 65 miles (104 km) of the Yalu River, the border between North Korea and the Chinese province of Manchuria.

The Chinese Communists had prepared their response. In October 1950 China entered the war on the side of North Korea. At first only relatively small Chinese forces were sent in to try out the task of fighting UN forces. But as the UN advance continued,

THE UN COMMAND

The United Nations Command (UNC) was the official name of the UN forces in Korea. Set up by the UN Security Council on July 7, 1950, the UNC was headed by the United States, which provided the vast majority of the forces engaged in resisting the North Korean invasion. The supreme commanders in Korea, first General Douglas MacArthur and then General Matthew Ridgway, were American and saw themselves as primarily responsible to the U.S. president, Harry S Truman, and to the joint chiefs of staff in the Pentagon (Department of Defense).

Fifteen other nations contributed troops to the UNC. They were allowed to fight under either the UN flag or their national flags. The Korean War was the first time the UN had authorized a military force to intervene to resist an act of aggression. The only similar operation with such a degree of UN support since Korea was the Persian Gulf War against Iraq in 1991.

The Korean War was sparked by the North's invasion of the South in June 1950. With UN support the North's attacks were defeated, but the Chinese sent their troops to support the North, and the UN forces were, in turn, forced to retreat. The war became bogged down into stalemate by June 1951, but small-scale fighting continued until an agreement was reached in July 1953. Korea was left divided in two.

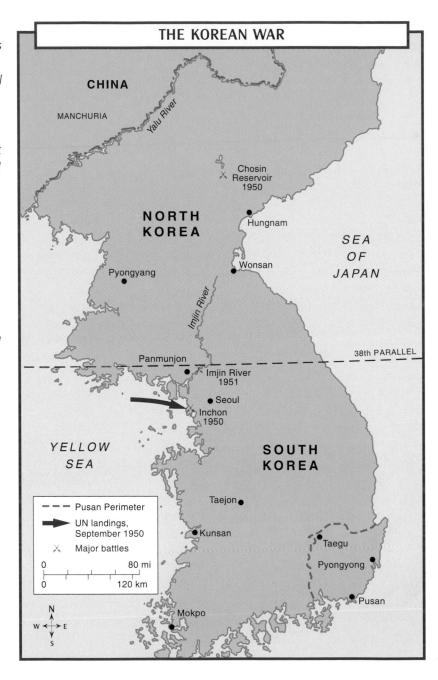

Chinese troops (the "People's Volunteers") had already begun secretly crossing the Yalu River. By November 25, a massive army of about 300,000 troops had surrounded the UN troops. With no tanks or air support, the Chinese relied on mass attacks. Their infantrymen were ordered to advance on the UN troops regardless of casualties. MacArthur's men were overwhelmed by surprise and the enemy's skill in night fighting—and their great numbers. Soon, demoralized UN troops were fleeing southward.

However, some units fought back well. For example, the U.S. 1st Marine Division led by General Oliver Smith was surrounded by eight Chinese divisions in the Chosin Reservoir area. Smith and his troops carried out an epic fighting retreat in the face of repeated attacks and bitterly cold winter weather between November 27 and December 9.

Grinding the enemy down

Eventually, the Chinese advance ran out of steam as their supply lines stretched to breaking point. Short of food, ammunition, and reinforcements, they came to a halt about 45 miles (72 km) south of Seoul. On January 25, 1951, the UN launched a counterattack. This time the UN forces used their massive firepower, both artillery and airstrikes, to overwhelming effect. The UN "meatgrinder," as this massive use of firepower became known, inflicted more casualties than even the Chinese could sustain. From January to March 1951, the UN troops ground their way back to the 38th Parallel. They recaptured Seoul on March 14.

An American soldier searches a Chinese prisoner who is being watched over by a member of the South Korean armed forces.

Totally committed to victory, MacArthur now wanted to raise the stakes again. He not only intended a renewed invasion of North Korea, but wanted to blockade mainland China, attack Chinese bases and industries in Manchuria, and use Nationalist Chinese troops from Formosa (now Taiwan) against the Communists. He even contemplated the use of the atom bomb to force the Chinese to quit the war. But MacArthur's political masters in Washington had had enough of MacArthur's challenges to the president's Constitutional authority. On April 11 he was replaced as commander by General Matthew Ridgway.

Stalemate and negotiations

By the end of May 1951, the war had reached stalemate. A Communist counteroffensive at the end of April had failed after heroic resistance by the British 29th Brigade, and especially the British Gloucestershire Regiment, at the Imjin River. A last Chinese offensive in May failed to penetrate beyond the 38th Parallel. The front stabilized roughly along the line of the prewar border between North and South Korea. Both sides made raids and conducted artillery bombardments, but there were no full-scale battles. Peace negotiations were opened the following July.

It took two years for negotiators to agree to an armistice, which was signed on July 27, 1953. Many thousands had died during the discussions. The situation in Korea returned to almost

General Douglas MacArthur (seated) visits one of the UN frontline units in South Korea. Behind him sits General Matthew Ridgway, who was to take over from MacArthur as the UN's supreme commander in South Korea in April 1951.

Watched by a South Korean child, U.S. troops prepare to board their trucks to head up to the front line. Once the fighting became stalemated, UN troops dug in, building lines of fortifications and trenches to defend the ground they had recaptured from the North Koreans and their Chinese ally.

exactly what it had been before the war broke out, with Korea divided between a Communist North and a pro-American South. The Korean War cost the lives of about 84,000 UN and South Korean troops. The cost in North Korean and Chinese casualties cannot be accurately counted, but was probably between one and two million killed and wounded. However, tensions in the region did not end with the 1953 armistice. Both North and South Korea continue to maintain an uneasy peace to the present.

UN COMMANDERS IN KOREA

On April 11, 1951, General Douglas MacArthur was dismissed from his command in the Far East. MacArthur was a hero in the United States and his dismissal caused a wave of public protest. But the disagreements between MacArthur on the one hand and President Harry S Truman and the U.S. joint chiefs of staff on the other were fundamental.

MacArthur was a headstrong military man with contempt for the idea of running the war by committee from Washington. He wanted to win victory in Korea at almost any cost and repeatedly made public his view that the U.S. government was hampering the war effort by the limits it placed on military action.

MacArthur's replacement as commander, General Matthew Ridgway, had already proved himself an outstanding leader. In Janaury 1951, he had halted the Chinese offensive and then launched his own successful counterattack, which threw the Chinese back into North Korea.

Wars of Liberation

At the end of World War II, Britain, France, Portugal, Belgium, and the Netherlands still possessed colonial empires, mostly in Africa and Asia. The authority of the European powers had been severely shaken by the events of the war, however. What is more, the two superpowers of the postwar world, the United States and the Soviet Union, were both in their different ways opposed to the continuation of European colonial rule. Over the following decades the European powers would lose the vast majority of their colonies.

In the 30 years between 1945 and 1975, the European powers gave up all but a few remnants of their empires. In some cases, this retreat from empire was a reasonably dignified transfer to designated successors. But in other cases it happened only after nationalists (local peoples opposed to being ruled by foreign powers) employing guerrilla or terror tactics had fought bitter campaigns against the colonial authorities. These campaigns forced European armies to develop their own new techniques of warfare, known collectively as counterinsurgency (COIN).

The French fought two major colonial wars against nationalist insurgents (rebels). The first was in Indochina (see pages 10–13). The second was in Algeria and began in 1954, just as the

Recruits to the Algerian National Liberation Front undergo weapons training. This body was dedicated to gaining independence from France and waged a successful campaign between 1954 and 1962. Many of the NLF's best soldiers had, in fact, received their training while serving with France's armed forces.

Indochina War was drawing to a close. A massive territory in North Africa, Algeria was technically not a colony, but a part of France. It was dominated by about a million European settlers, known as *pieds noirs*. The other 90 percent of the population were either Arab or Berber Muslims.

When a few hundred members of the Algerian nationalist Front de Libération Nationale (FLN—National Liberation Front) formed by a group of radical Muslims, began a campaign in Algeria on November 1, 1954, it seemed to pose little threat to French authority. In 1956 France granted independence to Algeria's nearest neighbors, Tunisia, and Morocco, but felt it could hold on to Algeria itself. FLN fighters were later able to use Tunisia as a safe haven, forcing the French to build a barrier, the Morice Line, to stop them from crossing between the two countries.

A brutal war

The FLN rapidly built up support among the Muslim population, who were not unnaturally tired of being treated as second-class citizens in their own country. There were brutal massacres and counter-massacres, as the FLN attacked *pied noir* families, and the *pieds noirs* and the French army retaliated with random attacks against Muslims. The FLN became secretly established in the Muslim casbah (old market) area of the Algerian capital, Algiers, and from its warren of narrow streets and small houses carried out terrorist attacks in the European part of the city.

In January 1957, paratrooper commander General Jacques Massu was ordered to clear Algiers of FLN terrorists. Massu carried out a campaign that was, on the face of it, highly successful. In what has become known as the Battle of Algiers, he saturated the casbah with troops, who carried out house-to-house searches for FLN fighters and weapons, and set up checkpoints at key

THE MORICE LINE

A barrier built by the French along Algeria's border with Tunisia, the Morice Line was 200 miles (320 km) long, stretching from the Mediterranean coast in the north to the wastes of the Sahara Desert in the south. The barrier consisted of an electrified fence at the center of a wide cleared strip, which was sown with antipersonnel mines and strung with barbed wire. Alongside the barrier was a dirt track regularly patrolled by French units.

Determined nationalist guerrillas could find a way through this barrier at night, but not without triggering electric sensors that alerted the French. Artillery fire and armored car patrols were immediately moved to the guerrilla crossing point. Helicopter-borne paratrooper units ranged over the area behind the fence, picking off any guerrillas who made it through. The Morice Line was extremely effective in preventing guerrilla penetration of Algeria from Tunisia. However, it tied up 80,000 French troops on border duties, allowing the internal revolt elsewhere in Algeria to grow unchecked.

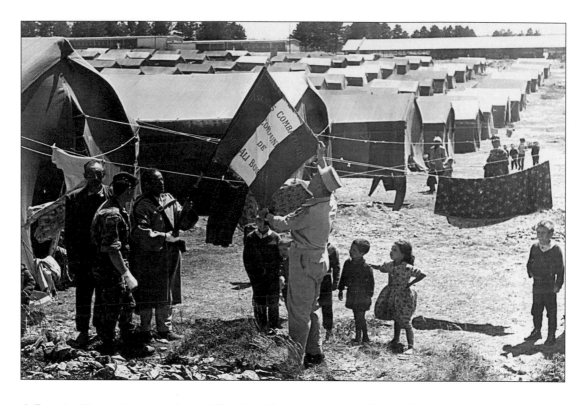

A French officer raises his unit's flag over a relocation camp in Algeria. A large number of Algerians were moved from their homes by the French. The French security forces were trying to deny the guerrillas the support offered by those Algerians who backed their cause.

points. The intelligence gained from these measures was supported by the questioning of FLN suspects, often involving the use of torture. Massu was able to build up a detailed picture of the FLN network in Algiers, and then move in to destroy it. But the brutality of Massu's methods, especially the use of torture, provoked widespread criticism in France and began to undermine France's political will to resist the Algerian nationalists.

Early French successes

There appeared to be no doubt about France's military ability to take on the FLN. Guerrillas operating inside Algeria were subject to an intense counterinsurgency offensive. One of the first measures taken was the mass relocation of Muslims from areas under guerrilla influence. As many as two million people may have been shifted to regions under the control of the French army. Then the French launched a series of large-scale search-and-destroy operations, sweeping through guerrilla strongholds.

By 1960 the FLN's military wing, the Armée de Libération Nationale (ALN—National Liberation Army) survived only in remote mountain regions. With about 500,000 heavily armed

French troops deployed, along with some 150,000 anti-ALN militiamen, the authorities had the military situation well in hand. But the political situation had slid into a disastrous confrontation between French army officers and *pieds noirs* on one side and the French government on the other.

French political leaders had become on the whole desperate to end the war in Algeria. The cost of the war in men and money was more than the French people would willingly bear. The manner in which this war of torture and massacre was being waged also caused much unfavorable reaction in France. But the French army leaders in Algeria and the *pieds noirs* themselves were totally committed to keeping Algeria French.

In May 1958, with the cooperation of some French army officers, the *pieds noirs* seized control of Algerian cities. They demanded a French government committed to French Algeria. The army officers even considered flying troops to Paris, the capital of France, to take power and install a military government. Under this pressure, the French Fourth Republic (the government) collapsed and the French general Charles de Gaulle, a hero of World War II, became president of a new government.

De Gaulle soon began to favor the idea of self-government for Algeria. He vigorously suppressed attempted army revolts in Algeria in 1960 and 1961. Despite a terrorist campaign by the Organisation Armée Secrète (OAS—Secret Army Organization), a group dedicated to keeping Algeria French, De Gaulle negotiated with the FLN and reached an agreement on Algerian independence in March 1962.

Britain's colonial wars

The British in their Southeast Asian colony of Malaya showed how a counterinsurgency campaign could be fought and won. The Malayan Emergency, as the campaign is known, lasted from 1948 to 1960. The Malayan Communist Party (MCP) launched a major guerrilla campaign in 1948. The Communists had some support among the colony's ethnic Chinese (people of Chinese descent) living in Malaya, a large minority who made up about 40 percent of the country's total

Members of a British patrol and a local tracker search for signs of guerrillas fighting for the Malayan Communist party, which was trying to end Britain's rule of Malaya. The campaign against the MCP lasted from 1948 to 1960. The British were able to defeat the MCP, but Malaya was granted its independence in 1957, becoming Malaysia.

population. Malays, on the other hand, were almost wholly united in their opposition to the guerrilla uprising. So the MCP could, at best, count on some support from only a minority of the Malayan population.

The MCP's guerrilla forces, known as the Malayan Races' Liberation Army, first tried to establish bases in populated areas, but these proved too vulnerable to counterattack by the British colonial forces. The guerrillas soon withdrew to bases in remote jungle areas, where they easily evaded sweeps by large-scale British army formations. The jungle was a difficult environment for the guerrillas, however. They only survived through support from Chinese "squatters." These were Chinese who, during the

MALAYA'S PROTECTED VILLAGES

A British doctor treats a Chinese family in one of Malaya's protected "New Villages." These villages denied Communist guerrillas the support of Malaya's ethnic Chinese.

General Sir Harold Briggs, the British director of operations in Malaya from 1950 to 1951, decided that support for the Communist guerrillas could only be undermined by moving some 423,000 Chinese "squatters" out of their villages on the edge of the Malayan jungle. Remarkably, this policy did not in general provoke a hostile reaction. Many squatters were resettled in "New Villages," where they lived behind barbed-wire fences under close police surveillance.

The British authorities made sure, however, that these protected villages had a good standard of housing and other facilities, making them a much better environment than the squatter villages on the jungle fringe. The squatters had generally not been especially attached to their crude dwellings and were often glad to be freed from the threats posed by the Communist guerrillas. The resettlement officers who ran the New Villages seem to have become genuinely popular figures.

INTELLIGENCE-GATHERING

The secret of the British success in Malaya was intelligence. This was carried out by the police Special Branch, which collected information from captured documents, civilian informers, surveillance work, and the questioning of prisoners. This information was passed to the army and used in counterinsurgency operations. The Special Branch concentrated in particular on identifying villagers who were arranging for the supply of food to guerrillas sheltering in the jungle.

When a supplier was identified, he was usually "turned"–guaranteed his freedom on condition he worked for the authorities. The supplier would continue to provide the guerrillas with food, but at the same time keep Special Branch informed of their whereabouts.

Captured guerrillas were also "turned" to work for the British and sent back into the jungle, where they either persuaded their companions to surrender or betrayed them to the authorities.

hardships of the Great Depression of the 1930s and the Japanese occupation of Malaya in 1941–45, had taken refuge in unoccupied land on the fringes of the jungle. Their villages were almost completely out of government control, and were a source of food, medicine, and recruits for the guerrillas.

Firm British action

The Communists carried out a sustained campaign of terrorist attacks and sabotage that especially targeted members of the local police forces and European managers of rubber plantations and tin mines. By 1950 the security situation was deteriorating and new policies were clearly required. General Sir Harold Briggs was appointed director of operations. Under his guidance coordinated action by the police, the army, and the civilian authorities replaced a purely military effort against the guerrillas. There was an emphasis on intelligence-gathering and small army units were sent out to hit identified guerrilla targets. The British authorities also began relocating the Chinese squatters, who numbered over 400,000, in protected villages where they would be under the control of the authorities.

After General Sir Gerald Templer was appointed High Commissioner of Malaya and commander-in-chief in 1952, these military policies were intensified. A declared state of emergency in Malaya gave the British extensive powers, including arrest without trial, the use of curfews, and compulsory identity cards. Templer divided the country into "black" zones where guerrillas were active and "white" zones where they were not. As an area was transformed from black to white, the emergency regulations were lifted, and the security forces were moved out, thereby restoring life back to normal.

Winning hearts and minds

By the mid-1950s, it was clear that the British counterinsurgency effort was proving a great success. The British enjoyed certain accidental advantages in Malaya. The guerrillas had no friendly neighboring country to supply arms, food, and safe bases. They were restricted to one small ethnic group that had little support among the majority of the population. But much of Britain's positive result was owed to the idea that, in Templer's words, the answer to guerrilla activity lay "not in pouring more troops into the jungle, but in the hearts and minds of the people."

The Chinese squatters, for example, were given better services and conditions of life in the protected villages where they were relocated. This soon turned them against the guerrillas. The use of minimum military force avoided the random unintentional injuring of civilians and destruction of their property that might

Kenyan militiamen, armed and equipped by the British colonial authorities, head out on patrol. Not all Kenyans supported the Mau Mau guerrillas, and many were targets of terrorist attacks. The buildings behind the patrol have been protected against the Mau Mau with stakes and barbed wire.

have driven people into the arms of the Communists. The British also pursued a political solution along with their counterinsurgency effort, ending with granting independence to Malaya in 1957.

Britain's other major counterinsurgency success of the 1950s was in the East African colony of Kenya, where a guerrilla movement known as the Mau Mau, based on the Kikuyu tribe, led to the declaration of a state of emergency in 1952. Measures such as the mass relocation of Kikuyu in protected villages and ruthless sweeps of country areas, which were treated as what would later be called "free fire zones" (anyone, however innocent, was considered a legitimate target and could be shot) brought the rebellion under control by 1956.

The counterinsurgency war in Kenya was a bloody affair, however. Around 12,000 Kikuyu were killed in the defeat of the guerrilla movement. One Kikuyu, Jomo Kenyatta, arrested by the British as a suspected Mau Mau leader, later became president of independent Kenya and a respected world statesman.

British forces also fought, with mixed success, against nationalists in Palestine, Cyprus, Aden, and Oman. By the end of the 1960s, Britain, like France, the Netherlands, and Belgium, had effectively accomplished a retreat from empire. In the 1970s the remaining nationalist anti-colonial insurgencies were concentrated in Africa—chiefly in the Portuguese colonies and in white-dominated southern Africa.

Portuguese troops on patrol in the jungles of Angola. The Portuguese faced a variety of guerrilla groups in the country and fought a bitter war there until they were forced to grant the West African country its full independence in 1975.

The last colonial powers

Portugal was the weakest of the European colonial powers, but the most determined to keep its colonies at all costs. By 1964 the Portuguese faced armed independence movements in all of their African territories—Guinea-Bissau (then Portuguese Guinea), Angola in West Africa, and Mozambique in southern Africa. Although short of money, equipment, and manpower to defend these colonies, Portugal refused to negotiate a withdrawal with any of the independence movements. By the early 1970s about 150,000 Portuguese soldiers, over 75 percent of the country's total army, were deployed in Africa.

The most successful of the liberation movements in the Portuguese colonies was the PAIGC (Partido Africano da Independencia da Guine e Cabo Verde—African Party for the Independence of Guinea and Cape Verde) in Guinea-Bissau. By 1973 the PAIGC had established control over large areas of the colony and announced an independent republic, although the Portuguese continued to resist a total takeover. The guerrilla fighters in Mozambique—Frelimo (Frente de Libertaçao de Mozambique, Mozambique Liberation Front)—and the guerrillas fighting in Angola had less success.

In April 1974, however, a popular revolution in Portugal overthrew the government and established a new regime committed to a rapid end to the African wars. Guinea-Bissau became independent on September 10, 1974, and independence for Angola and Mozambique followed in 1975.

Wars in southern Africa

Independence did not bring peace to Angola and Mozambique. They became involved in a struggle over the future of the region. Since the 1960s guerrillas had been struggling for independence in Angola's southern neighbor, Namibia, a country that was controlled by the white-dominated Republic of South Africa. There were also two guerrilla movements opposing white minority rule in Rhodesia (now Zimbabwe), whose colonists had declared their independence from Britain in 1965. The collapse of Portuguese rule in Angola and Mozambique threatened to undermine white control of both Namibia and Rhodesia. In South Africa's view, it also threatened a Communist takeover of all southern Africa.

Even before the Portuguese had officially left Angola, the country was plunged into a civil war in which outside powers quickly intervened. Three independence movements all claimed to be the legitimate government. One, which controlled the capital, Luanda, was backed by the Soviet Union and Cuba. By January 1976 Cuba had sent about 13,000 troops into the country. The other two were backed by the United States and South Africa. South African troops advanced on Luanda from the south and U.S.-backed mercenaries invaded Angola from Zaire.

The Cubans proved effective, crushing the mercenary advance and driving back the South Africans. But the Angolan guerrilla group backed by the Cubans could not establish control of all of Angola. One of its rivals for power, backed by South Africa and the United States, kept control of much of the south and center.

MERCENARIES

Bands of white mercenaries (soldiers fighting for money not a cause) became important in Africa during and after the withdrawal of the colonial powers. Local military forces were often so weak that a few well-armed mercenary troops led by bold officers could have a decisive impact.

Mercenaries first appeared in the former Belgian Congo in the 1960s, where independence was followed by a series of confused civil conflicts. British, French, and Belgian officers recruited men, mostly from Rhodesia and South Africa, on behalf of various parties in the Congolese wars. At one point, in 1967, some mercenaries even planned to take over the Congo themselves, but the attempt was a complete failure.

Mercenaries were later recruited to fight in the Nigerian Civil War of 1967-70, and in Angola in 1976. The Angolan adventure ended disastrously for the mercenaries, who soon broke up when faced with properly armed and trained Cuban forces. Some were captured, tried, and imprisoned or executed.

White mercenaries fighting in the civil war in the Congo in the 1960s. Although few in number, they played an important part in the war.

Establishing peace in southern Africa was a slow and painful process. The first major step was a cease-fire in Rhodesia in December 1979. The country became independent, under black majority rule, on April 18, 1980. South Africa then redoubled its efforts to keep hold of Namibia and ensure that Angola and Mozambique were weakened by civil war. The South Africans promoted an immensely destructive guerrilla campaign against the Frelimo government in Mozambique. South African forces also made repeated armed raids into southern Angola between 1980 and 1984.

Eventually, in 1988, agreement was reached on independence for Namibia and a withdrawal of Cuban forces from Angola. This was the beginning of a general movement toward peace in southern Africa, which culminated in the removal of white rule in South Africa itself in 1994.

ARAB AND ISRAELI WARS

The creation of the Jewish state of Israel in May 1948 triggered off a cycle of conflicts that still has not run its course. The foundation of Israel was a result of the determination of Jewish Zionists, members of a group founded in 1896 to promote the establishment of a Jewish state in Palestine, their ancient homeland. After World War I, Zionists based their claim on the 1917 Balfour Declaration committing Britain to support such a state. Arabs in the Middle East never accepted the right of the Jews to set up a state on what they saw as Arab land.

By 1947 the British, who had controlled Palestine since World War I, could no longer govern the region in the face of Jewish and Arab terrorism (see page 50). The United Nations intervened to end the violence. The UN decided that Palestine should be divided into a Jewish and an Arab state, but the Arabs rejected this solution. On May 14, 1948, therefore, Jewish leaders declared their part of Palestine independent and named the new state Israel. Israel was immediately invaded by the Arab states of Egypt, Syria, Iraq, Lebanon, and Transjordan (now Jordan).

An Israeli jeep moves through the Negev Desert during the 1948 war against various neighboring Arab states. Despite being heavily outnumbered, the Israelis were able to defeat the Arab states one by one, ensuring that the new state of Israel would survive.

On the face of it, this first war between the Jews and their Arab neighbors was an unequal struggle that the Israelis should have lost. But the Israeli Defense Forces (IDF) had the advantage of defending a small area with good internal communications and many Israelis had had military training in self-defense groups created to protect them from Arab attacks. Since the Arab attacks were largely uncoordinated, the Israelis were able to switch their forces between the different fronts to meet each threat as it arose. The Israelis also soon began to receive considerable quantities of modern military equipment.

Israel survives

During the first month of fighting, the Israelis won control of the northern part of the Jordan River, driving off the Syrians and Lebanese advancing from the north and the Iraqis in the west. On June 11, the United Nations arranged a truce (temporary end to the fighting), but this was broken a month later when the Egyptians attacked on the southern front. The IDF successfully held off the Egyptians in some of the heaviest fighting of the war, while at the same time launching its own offensives against the Syrians in Galilee and the Jordanians around the city of Jerusalem.

By mid-July, when a second truce came into effect, the Israelis had thoroughly taken the strategic lead. They used the break in the fighting to further build up their arms and to organize for a decisive attack. On October 28, the IDF went on the offensive in Galilee, on the Lebanon border, clearing the area of Arab forces in three days. The Israelis were then able to concentrate all their forces on the Egyptians. They seized control of the Negev Desert and invaded Egyptian territory at Abu Aweigila on December 27.

International pressure forced the Israelis to pull back from invading Egypt itself, but they had clearly won the war. Divided and demoralized, the Arab states agreed to armistices with Israel between February 24 and July 20, 1949. The armistice lines

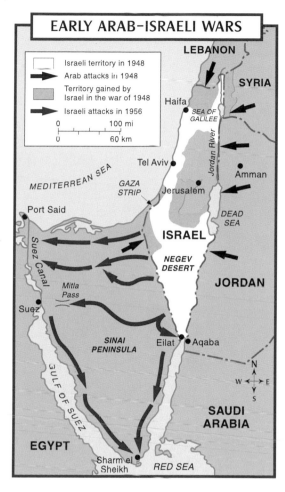

EARLY ARAB-ISRAELI WARS

- ☐ Israeli territory in 1948
- → Arab attacks in 1948
- ▨ Territory gained by Israel in the war of 1948
- → Israeli attacks in 1956

0 — 100 mi
0 — 60 km

LEBANON
SYRIA
Haifa
SEA OF GALILEE
Jordan River
MEDITERREAN SEA
Tel Aviv
Amman
GAZA STRIP
Jerusalem
Port Said
DEAD SEA
ISRAEL
NEGEV DESERT
JORDAN
Suez Canal
Mitla Pass
Suez
SINAI PENINSULA
Eilat • Aqaba
N
W ← → E
S
GULF OF SUEZ
SAUDI ARABIA
EGYPT
Sharm el Sheikh
RED SEA

The Israelis went to war with their Arab neighbors twice between the late 1940s and 1950s. First, in 1948 to preserve their new state and second in 1956 as part of a plan to weaken the regime of Egyptian leader Gamal Abdel Nasser.

became, in effect, the borders of the new state. Israel now consisted of the part of Palestine originally allotted to the Jews under the UN's 1947 partition plan, plus half of Jerusalem and areas on the Lebanese border to the north and the Egyptian border in the south. Jordan remained in occupation of the West Bank of the Jordan River and the eastern section of Jerusalem, and Egypt held the Gaza Strip.

The first Arab-Israeli conflict left an unstable situation. None of the Arab states recognized Israel's right to exist. They persisted in seeing the Israeli state as an illegal occupant of Arab territory. Hundreds of thousands of Palestinian Arabs had fled from their homes in what was now Israel, and lived as stateless refugees in camps around Israel's borders. The Israelis, for their part, saw their territory as impossibly hard to defend, and looked for a chance to expand Israel's borders to more defensible lines.

Superpower involvement

In 1952, a group of military officers seized power in Egypt. Two years later one of the officers, Gamal Abdel Nasser, emerged as a powerful leader. In July 1956, Nasser announced the Egyptian takeover of the Suez Canal, which was owned by Britain and France. The canal was a vital route between the European powers and the Far East. The British and French responded by making a secret agreement with Israel to attack Egypt.

British warships, landing barges, and troop-carrying helicopters head for Port Said at the beginning of their invasion of Egypt in November 1956. The attack was the first time in military history that helicopters had been used to move large number of troops into battle.

ARIEL SHARON AT THE MITLA PASS

At the start of the Israeli assault on Sinai on October 29, 1956, one battalion of the 202nd Parachute Brigade, commanded by Colonel Ariel Sharon, seized the east end of the Mitla Pass in an airborne assault.

The rest of the brigade, supported by a small force of tanks, forced its way overland through the 190 miles (304 km) from the Israeli border to Mitla, overcoming Egyptian opposition as they went. It took 28 hours to join up with the airborne force. Holding the east end of the pass, the parachute brigade had fulfilled its objective, controlling a vital route between Suez and central Sinai. However, Sharon was not content with this success. He sent his men forward to capture the rest of the Mitla Pass. This they achieved, but only after heavy fighting against Egyptian troops hidden in caves and hollows along the sides of the narrow passage.

The paratroops suffered what were by Israeli standards heavy casualties–38 dead and 120 wounded. Sharon was severely criticized for this unnecessary action.

On October 29, 1956, the IDF invaded Sinai and advanced on the Suez Canal. This was the prearranged excuse for Britain and France to attack Egypt and seize control of the canal, allegedly to protect the international waterway from the fighting. By November 5, the Israelis had complete control of the Sinai peninsula. British and French paratroopers dropped into the Port Said area and, the following day, the French and British forces made landings at the Mediterranean end of the canal.

An uneasy peace

But France and Britain had failed to take into account the global balance of power. Their action was condemned by both the Soviet Union and the United States as an example of outdated colonialism and a clear violation of Egyptian independence. International pressure forced them to accept a cease-fire on November 7. The French, British, and Israeli forces were withdrawn from Egypt under the supervision of UN monitors.

For the next ten years Arabs and Israelis lived side by side in an uneasy peace. It was a time of important changes in the region, however. The major anti-Israel Arab states, Egypt and Syria, won the backing of the Soviet Union, while the United States became gradually drawn into supporting Israel. The Israeli economy flourished and the country grew in population and in

The wreckage of an Egyptian column in the Sinai peninsula after it had been attacked by Israeli aircraft during the Six-Days War in 1967. Absolute command of the air was central to Israel's rapid defeat of its Arab neighbors.

military strength. Many Palestinian Arabs ceased to believe that the Arab states would ever defeat Israel and restore Palestine to Arab rule. One militant Palestinian, Yassir Arafat, created a guerrilla movement, Al Fatah, to carry out armed raids on Israel. In 1964, the Arab states themselves created the Palestinian Liberation Organization (PLO), which became the coordinating body for anti-Israeli Arab commando groups.

In 1967 guerrilla raids on Israel and Israeli counterstrikes against guerrilla bases in neighboring Arab countries increased. Both sides began to feel that a new military showdown was approaching. Egypt took the initiative. In May Nasser sent his troops into Sinai, ordered UN observers to quit the border with Israel, and declared the closing of the Strait of Tiran to Israeli shipping. Israel decided to attack immediately.

Israel's first strike

In the early hours of June 5, 1967, the Israeli Air Force (IAF) attacked Egyptian air bases to devastating effect. Almost the entire Egyptian Air Force was knocked out in two hours. The IAF then turned its attention to Egypt's allies, Jordan and Syria, inflicting similar damage on their aircraft. With complete command of the air, the Israelis crushed the Egyptian army in the Sinai peninsula, winning a series of desert tank battles against numerically superior armored forces. By June 9, the Israelis were in control of the east bank of the Suez Canal.

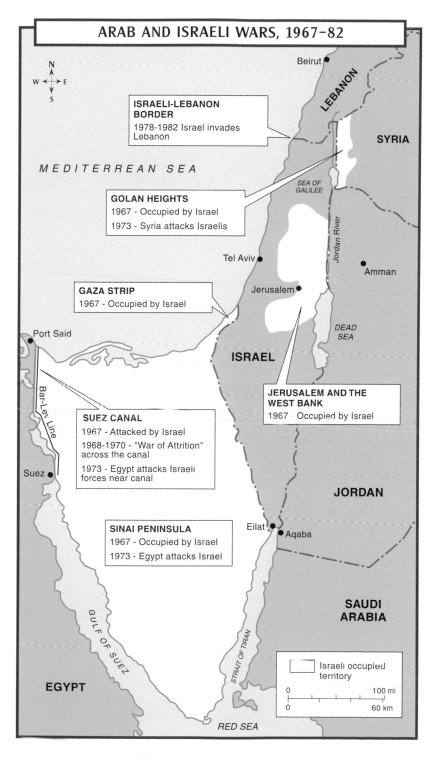

ARAB AND ISRAELI WARS, 1967–82

N
W ← → E
S

Beirut

ISRAELI-LEBANON BORDER
1978-1982 Israel invades Lebanon

LEBANON

SYRIA

MEDITERREAN SEA

SEA OF GALILEE

GOLAN HEIGHTS
1967 - Occupied by Israel
1973 - Syria attacks Israelis

Jordan River

Tel Aviv

Amman

GAZA STRIP
1967 - Occupied by Israel

Jerusalem

DEAD SEA

ISRAEL

Port Said

JERUSALEM AND THE WEST BANK
1967 - Occupied by Israel

Bar-Lev Line

SUEZ CANAL
1967 - Attacked by Israel
1968-1970 - "War of Attrition" across the canal
1973 - Egypt attacks Israeli forces near canal

Suez

JORDAN

SINAI PENINSULA
1967 - Occupied by Israel
1973 - Egypt attacks Israel

Eilat
Aqaba

SAUDI ARABIA

GULF OF SUEZ

STRAIT OF TIRAN

Israeli occupied territory

0   100 mi
0   60 km

EGYPT

RED SEA

Israel was involved in two major wars with its Arab neighbors between 1967 and 1982, as well as a number of smaller conflicts. There were major wars in 1967 and 1973. Israel was overwhelmingly successful in 1967 but had to fight hard to win in 1973. The war in 1973 was the last major conflict in the region, bul bouts of fighting broke out in the following decades.

Meanwhile, the Jordanians had launched an offensive on June 5 in support of the Egyptians. After some hard fighting the Israelis drove the Jordanians back and, on the 7th, took control of the whole of the West Bank and Jerusalem. The IDF was now free to turn its attention to the Syrians, who were occupying fortified positions on the Golan Heights, the hilly region of northern Israel, dominating Galilee. On June 9, a combined assault by Israeli infantry, tanks, and aircraft captured the Golan Heights and drove the Syrians back in disarray.

By June 10, the Six-Day War, as it became known, was over. It left Israel in occupation of the West Bank, the Golan Heights, the Gaza Strip, and Sinai. Military victory was not followed by political or diplomatic successes, however. The Arab states were left more embittered than ever, and more determined to fight Israel. The large Palestinian populations in the West Bank and Gaza presented a potentially serious security threat for the Israelis. The United Nations condemned the Israeli occupation of these areas and Sinai, increasing Israel's isolation and exclusive dependence on the United States.

Hostilities continue

The Six-Day War was not followed by peace. Egypt, flooded with new equipment by the Soviet Union, engaged in a "war of attrition" against Israel across the Suez Canal in 1969-70, which led to serious clashes in the air and on the ground. It was not outright war, but a campaign of air and artillery attacks, and small-scale clashes between troops. The Israelis built a number of fortifications, the Bar-Lev Line, to defend the east bank of the Suez Canal Meanwhile, Arafat's Al Fatah group became the dominant force in the PLO, and Palestinians began resorting to international terrorist attacks to publicize their cause (see pages 50–52).

THE BAR-LEV LINE

In March 1969 the Israeli forces occupying the Sinai peninsula completed the construction of a defensive fortification along the east bank of the Suez Canal. Stretching 100 miles (160 km) from the Mediterranean Sea to the Gulf of Suez, it was known as the Bar-Lev Line after the Israeli chief of staff, General Chaim Bar-Lev.

The line was a complex arrangement of bunkers, trenches, and strongpoints, designed to be manned by lightly armed infantry. Behind the line, two north-south roads were built to allow self-propelled artillery and armored vehicles to arrive rapidly in support of any point in the line that came under attack by the Egyptians.

When the Egyptians launched their Yom Kippur offensive across the Suez Canal in 1973, the Bar-Lev Line was undermanned and did not prove much of an obstacle to overcome. It has also been argued that the existence of the Bar-Lev Line contributed to Israeli confidence, making them less prepared for the serious battle they had on their hands in 1973.

CROSSING THE SUEZ CANAL

Early in the morning of October 6, 1973, Egyptian ground and air forces began an intensive bombardment of Israeli positions along the east bank of the Suez Canal. At the same time small units of Egyptian assault troops paddled across the canal in rubber boats. Although they came under fire from Israeli soldiers manning the Bar-Lev Line, most of the assault troops reached the east bank and set about destroying Israeli strongpoints. Further assault waves followed at regular intervals. By early evening the Egyptian troops had established a foothold about 5 miles (8 km) deep and were clearing gaps in the sand ramparts of the Bar-Lev Line.

Amphibious (land and sea) vehicles were soon heading across the canal in large numbers, while bridges were

assembled, each one taking only 30 minutes to put in place. By midnight, Egyptian tanks and artillery were in position on the east bank of the canal in support of the infantry. It was a well-planned operation that cost just 200 Egyptian lives.

A Soviet-supplied tank of the Egyptian army heads into the Sinai Desert after crossing the Suez Canal, October 1973.

In 1973, open war flared once more. On the Jewish holy day of Yom Kippur, October 6, Egypt and Syria attacked Israeli forces in Sinai on the Suez Canal and the Golan Heights respectively. The Egyptians quickly broke through the Bar-Lev Line, which was only lightly defended. Armed with the latest Soviet antitank and ground-to-air missiles, the Egyptian forces inflicted heavy losses on Israeli armor and aircraft, which counterattacked without due caution.

Meanwhile, similar fierce battles developed on the Golan Heights, where an early Syrian breakthrough was driven back by the Israelis, but once again at the cost of heavy casualties. The turning point of the Yom Kippur War came on October 14, when the Egyptians attempted an over-ambitious advance into the

Watched by local villagers, Israeli troops move into southern Lebanon, March 1978. The Israelis invaded in an attempt to destroy training bases from which Palestinian fighters had been launching raids into Israel.

heart of Sinai. The Israelis countered with devastating speed and power. They destroyed much of the Egyptian armor and, on October 15, established a foothold on the west bank of the Suez Canal. This cut off the Egyptian Third Army on the east bank of the canal and left Cairo, the Egyptian capital, apparently at Israel's mercy. At the same time, the IDF fought its way forward in Syria, threatening Damascus, the Syrian capital.

With the United States and the Soviet Union thoroughly committed to opposing sides in the war, it became essential to bring about a cease-fire to avoid the risk of a global war between the two superpowers. The Arab oil states had also begun to stop shipments of oil to Western Europe and North America. A cease-fire was agreed to on both fronts on October 22.

Although Israel had once more ended the victor, the Yom Kippur War was a severe blow to Israeli morale. Israeli losses of 1,854 dead were high by their standards The initial response to the war had revealed disturbing levels of complacency. The Arab states, on the other hand, had gained prestige.

After the Yom Kippur War much skillful diplomatic work brought peace at last between Egypt and Israel in the Camp David accords of 1978. This agreement was arranged by U.S. President Jimmy Carter between Israel's Prime Minister Menachim Begin and Egypt's President Anwar Sadat. The agreement was finalized at Camp David, the U.S. president's retreat in

Maryland, and signed in Washington, D.C., on March 26, 1979. But the key issue of the Palestinian Arabs, who were still demanding a homeland, remained an unresolved issue.

Lebanon invaded

The presence of large numbers of armed PLO fighters helped reduce Lebanon to a state of chaos and civil war from 1975. In March 1978, the Israelis carried out a sudden invasion of southern Lebanon in an attempt to destroy Palestinian guerrilla bases. However, the Palestinians withdrew farther north. The following month the Israelis withdrew, leaving a pro-Israeli militia behind to patrol a zone in southern Lebanon, where UN peacekeepers also took up position.

In June 1982, the Israelis embarked on a second, larger-scale invasion of Lebanon known as Operation Peace for Galilee. They advanced on three fronts, overwhelming Palestinian resistance. In eastern Lebanon, the IDF encountered Syrian forces that had been in Lebanon since 1976. The result was a devastating display of the superiority of the Israelis' latest American-supplied technology to the Syrians' Soviet-supplied hardware. Using highly developed electronic warfare equipment to identify Syrian targets

Israeli armored forces advance through southern Lebanon in U.S.-supplied vehicles at the beginning of Operation Peace for Galilee, June 1982.

Rescue workers and investigators survey the ruins of the U.S. barracks in Beirut destroyed by a Lebanese suicide bomber, October 1983.

and confuse their radar, Israel destroyed most of the Syrian air force and Syria's antiaircraft surface-to-air-missile (SAM) systems at hardly any cost to its own air force.

From mid-June, the IDF laid siege to the western part of Beirut, the headquarters of the PLO, which was defended by a mixture of Palestinians, Syrians, and Lebanese Muslims. The siege lasted for more than two months, during which the Israelis subjected the city to artillery and air bombardment. Eventually, an agreement was reached for the Palestinian fighters to evacuate Beirut under the supervision of a Multi-National Force (MNF). The evacuation was completed in August and the MNF withdrew on September 10. Four days later, the Israelis moved into the western section of Beirut. Israel's Lebanese Christian militia allies carried out a notorious massacre of defenseless Palestinian civilians in the refugee camps of Sabra and Chatila. The militia had been allowed into the camp by the Israelis to search for Palestinian terrorists, who may have played a part in the recent assassination of Lebanon's newly elected president.

The MNF was hurriedly redeployed on September 20, but its presence only contributed further to the savage chaos into which Lebanon descended over the following years. On October 23, 1983, 297 members of the U.S. and French MNF units were killed in Lebanese terrorist suicide attacks on their barracks. The MNF withdrew the following year. Israel also effected a slow, step-by-step withdrawal, although attempting to keep its control of a part of southern Lebanon along the border with Israel.

The search for peace continues

Through the 1980s it became increasingly clear that Israeli military superiority in the Middle East still could not guarantee peace and security for the Israeli state. In 1987 widespread disturbances began among the Palestinian population of the occupied territories of the West Bank and Gaza. This unrest, known as the Intifada, presented a new kind of challenge to Israeli soldiers, trying to maintain order and uphold authority in the face of stone-throwing youths and chanting demonstrators.

Faced with the prospect of endless civil disturbances and terrorist attacks, in 1993 the Israeli government of Prime Minister Yitzhak Rabin at last gambled on peace. Rabin and Arafat signed a U.S.-arranged peace agreement that was to give the Palestinians self-government in the West Bank and Gaza. In return, the PLO for the first time accepted Israel's right to exist.

Arafat was elected leader of the new Palestinian Authority in January 1996. However, Islamic extremists continued to carry out terrorist bombings. In April 1996, Israel retaliated by bombarding Lebanon, in one incident killing 100 Lebanese civilians. The assassination of Rabin by an Israeli extremist in 1995 was a reminder that some Israelis strongly opposed the peace process.

In October 1998 the Israeli leader Benjamin Netanyahu and Arafat met at Wye Mills, Maryland. Their discussions, arranged by President Bill Clinton, led to an agreement that Palestinian security forces, with U.S. aid, would crack down on Islamic extremist attacks on Israeli targets in return for the Israelis halting the building of Jewish settlements on the West Bank.

THE COLD WAR

The end of World War II in 1945 left the United States as overwhelmingly the strongest power in the world, both militarily and economically. Its only possible rival was the Soviet Union, which was a poverty-stricken, war-ruined state, but possessed powerful land and air forces that had driven forward into the heart of Europe. These two states, known as the superpowers, would struggle to gain influence around the world for the next four decades, bringing the world to the brink of nuclear war on several occasions.

In mid-1948 the Soviet Union stopped all ground traffic flowing between West Germany and West Berlin, which was in Soviet-controlled East Germany. Supply aircraft like these stopped West Berliners starving.

The United States and the Soviet Union had been allies during World War II, but their political differences quickly came to the surface once the fighting ended. The creation of Communist governments, which controlled the countries of Soviet-occupied Eastern Europe, between 1945 and 1947—actually single-party states based on the unrestrained power of their secret police forces—deeply offended American opinion. In March 1946, speaking in Fulton, Missouri, the former British Prime Minister Winston Churchill summed up the political division of Europe, talking of an "iron curtain" that was being erected by the Soviet Union across Europe.

THE TRUMAN DOCTRINE

During the winter of 1946–47, President Harry S Truman had to decide whether to resume America's policy of isolationism. Isolationism, the political policy of not becoming directly involved in overseas affairs that did not seemingly have any importance to the United States, had been abandoned in World War II.

Truman could have reduced America's armed forces and halted America's direct involvement in overseas events. But Truman was hostile to Communism and suspicious of the plans of the Soviet leader Joseph Stalin. When Britain declared itself no longer able to maintain the role of resisting Communist pressure on Greece and Turkey, countries vital to the security of the West, Truman agreed to take on the responsibility.

On March 12, 1947, Truman announced: "I believe it must be the policy of the United States to support free peoples who are resisting attempted subjugation by armed minorities or outside pressures." This "Truman Doctrine," committing the United States to resist the spread of Communism worldwide, whether occurring through an internal revolt or through pressure from Communist forces, governed American policy for the next 40 years.

In March 1947, President Harry S Truman committed the United States to preventing the spread of Communism. The first test of U.S. commitment came in 1948, when the Soviet Union blocked access to West Berlin, which had been occupied by U.S., British, and French forces since 1945, but lay within the Soviet-controlled East Germany. The Americans and British mounted an airlift which kept West Berlin supplied with food and fuel under difficult conditions from June 1948 until September 1949.

Forming rival alliances

The Soviet Union dropped its attempt to force the Western allies out of West Berlin in 1949, but the confrontation between East and West intensified. The North Atlantic Treaty Organization (NATO) was formed, linking the countries of Western Europe and the United States and Canada in a military alliance directed against the Soviet Union. The Soviet Union formed a similar alliance with the countries of Eastern Europe, the Warsaw Pact, in 1955. The news that the Soviet Union had tested its first atomic bomb in 1949 was followed by the fall of mainland China to Communists (see pages 5–9). These events raised American fears about Communism to a new pitch.

At the end of World War II in 1945, Europe was gradually divided into two zones–Western and Eastern Europe. Both were tied in military and political alliances that were intensely suspicious of each other. This division lasted until the late 1980s, when the conflict between the two power blocs ended because of the collapse of the Soviet Union.

A DIVIDED EUROPE

ICELAND

N
W ←↓→ E
S

NATO members, 1949-89

Warsaw Pact members, 1955-89

States belonging to neither military alliance

The Iron Curtain

NORTH SEA

NORWAY

SWEDEN

FINLAND

REP. OF IRELAND

GREAT BRITAIN

DENMARK

SOVIET UNION

ATLANTIC OCEAN

NETH.

BELG.

LUXEMBOURG

WEST GERMANY

EAST GERMANY

POLAND

CZECHOSLOVAKIA

SWITZERLAND

AUSTRIA

HUNGARY

FRANCE

YUGOSLAVIA

ROMANIA

PORTUGAL

ITALY

Corsica

BULGARIA

SPAIN

ALBANIA

Sardinia

GREECE

TURKEY

Sicily

0   500 mi
0   800 km

The following year the Korean War began (see pages 14–19), pitching the Western allies, under the UN banner, into open war against Communism. The U.S. government held back from using atomic weapons, however, and took measures to stop the war spreading. The Soviet Union supported both the North Koreans and their Chinese Communist backers in the fighting, but did not openly commit its own forces. Thus the pattern was set for the "Cold War." The United States and the Soviet Union would push their rivalry in every way possible, short of directly fighting one another. Both also equipped and trained other armies.

In the 1950s the two superpowers embarked on a nuclear arms race that was to last until 1987. At first, the two rivals concentrated on producing bigger and bigger bombs to be delivered to a target by long-range aircraft. The first hydrogen bomb, tested by the Americans in 1952, was soon matched by the Soviet

Union. By 1962 the Soviet Union exploded the largest bomb ever, delivering 58 megatons (a megaton is an explosive force equivalent to that of one million tons of the explosive TNT), which was equal to 3,000 of the original atom bombs used in World War II.

The focus of the arms race had, however, by then long shifted to the development of intercontinental ballistic missiles (ICBMs), generally delivering a smaller atomic bomb, but in far greater numbers and with a greater likelihood of getting through the enemy's defenses. The first effective ICBM, the American Atlas-D, was deployed in 1958. The following year the United States began deployment of submarine-launched Polaris ballistic missiles each with several nuclear warheads (the section of a missile containing the nuclear device). The Soviet Union proved it could match American developments, although mostly a step behind.

Mutual destruction

Strategic thinking developed along with the new weapons. By the mid-1960s, both the United States and the Soviet Union faced the prospect of seeing all their major cities and military bases wiped out within an hour of a war beginning. Both created elaborate early-warning systems, using satellites and ground-based sensors, to detect a nuclear strike by the other side as soon as it was launched. They planned to launch their own counterstrike before the enemy missiles arrived. This created nuclear deterrence known as MAD—Mutually Assured Destruction. In a MAD world, each side knew it could not afford to start a war, because it would itself be destroyed.

The nearest the superpowers came to nuclear war was the Cuban missile crisis of 1962. Cuba had been taken over by the guerrilla leader Fidel Castro in 1958. Castro soon declared himself a Communist and nationalized (took over) American

THE NUCLEAR THREAT

In the 1980s, the nuclear arsenals of the two superpowers contained a total explosive power of around 15,000 megatons. This was equivalent to 1.25 million atomic bombs of the kind dropped on the Japanese city of Hiroshima in 1945. It has been calculated that in the whole of human history, about 20 megatons of explosives have been used in warfare, so the 1980s nuclear arsenals constituted 750 times the total of explosives employed in all wars to date.

Figures for the probable loss of human life in a nuclear war between the superpowers varied widely, but the death of two billion people worldwide was not considered an exaggerated prediction. Some people believed it would end life on Earth. At the height of the Cold War this massive destructive power was held on a hair-trigger, since each of the superpowers was all set to launch a massive nuclear missile counterattack within minutes of being alerted to an attack by its enemy.

Fidel Castro (with raised arm) is welcomed into Havana, the Cuban capital, in January 1959 after his popular revolution led to the overthrow of the dictator General Fulgencio Batista. Castro's regime was backed by the Soviet Union, a situation that the United States could not tolerate. Cuba became a focal point of tension between the United States and the Soviet Union in the early part of the 1960s.

businesses. The United States responded by promoting an invasion of Cuba by anti-Castro Cuban exiles at the Bay of Pigs in April 1961. The invasion was a failure and left Castro triumphant.

Depending on the Soviet Union to defend him from American hostility, Castro welcomed a plan to place medium-range Soviet nuclear missiles in Cuba, from where they could hit targets in the United States. President John F. Kennedy saw this as an unacceptable shift in the strategic balance of power. On October 22, 1962, Kennedy declared a blockade of Cuba and began a test of wills with Soviet leader Nikita Khrushchev. Eventually, a deal was struck for the withdrawal of the missiles, but not before there were several moments when nuclear war came perilously close.

Ending the nuclear arms race

The Cuban missile crisis gave the superpower leaders a fright, and led to the first serious agreements to control the nuclear arms race. The testing of nuclear weapons in the atmosphere was banned. Nuclear arsenals continued to develop, however. In the 1970s, the introduction of missiles with multiple warheads vastly increased the number of targets that could be hit. Strategic Arms Limitations Talks (SALT) produced a first agreement in 1972, but their main effect was to allow the Soviet Union to catch up with the United States in its nuclear arsenal.

In the 1980s, new measures destabilized the nuclear balance. These included the siting of U.S. Cruise missiles with nuclear warheads in Europe and the "Star Wars" initiative. The "Star Wars" initiative, named after a series of successful science fiction movies, planned to give the United States the ability to defend itself from nuclear attack through space-based defense systems, and thus end the mutually assured destruction on which deterrence was based. Only the coming to power of reform-minded Mikhail Gorbachev as Soviet leader, dedicated to ending the Cold War, brought an end to the nuclear arms race in 1987.

Supporting friendly powers

Unable to fight a direct war because of nuclear deterrence, the superpowers devoted much of their time to espionage and propaganda. The American Central Intelligence Agency (CIA), created in 1947, grew to be a massive organization, not only spying on the Soviet Union and its allies, but carrying out subversive operations against left-wing regimes and even planning the assassination of pro-Communist leaders. The Soviet secret police, the KGB, fought against the CIA throughout the Cold War.

The Cold War was a global conflict fought from just after World War II to the late 1980s The United States and the Soviet Union, and their allies, tried to defend their spheres of influence.

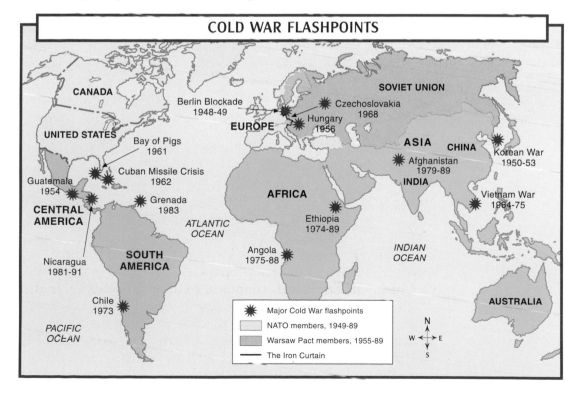

COLD WAR FLASHPOINTS

CANADA

UNITED STATES

Berlin Blockade
1948-49

Czechoslovakia
1968

Hungary
1956

EUROPE

SOVIET UNION

ASIA

CHINA

Korean War
1950-53

Bay of Pigs
1961

Afghanistan
1979-89

INDIA

Guatemala
1954

Cuban Missile Crisis
1962

AFRICA

Vietnam War
1964-75

CENTRAL
AMERICA

Grenada
1983

ATLANTIC
OCEAN

Ethiopia
1974-89

INDIAN
OCEAN

Nicaragua
1981-91

SOUTH
AMERICA

Angola
1975-88

Chile
1973

AUSTRALIA

PACIFIC
OCEAN

Major Cold War flashpoints
NATO members, 1949-89
Warsaw Pact members, 1955-89
The Iron Curtain

N
W — E
S

Soviet tanks take up position on the streets of the Hungarian capital, Budapest, in 1956. The people of Hungary, a Soviet-controlled state in Eastern Europe, tried to win their freedom, but the Soviet Union acted quickly, sending its forces into the country to end the uprising.

The conflict between the superpowers obliged almost every country in the world to align itself with one or the other. Since India established close relations with the Soviet Union, for example, its regional rival Pakistan ended up as an ally of the United States. Newly independent countries across the world, freed from European colonial rule in the 1950s and 1960s, slipped into either the U.S. or the Soviet camp.

Protecting areas of influence

Direct intervention by the superpowers was largely devoted not to changing the existing conditions, but to maintaining their hold on areas regarded as within their respective spheres of influence. The Soviet Union sent tanks into Hungary in 1956 to crush an anti-Communist uprising, and into Czechoslovakia in 1968 to remove a liberal Communist government. The Soviet invasion of Afghanistan in 1979 was an attempt to prevent the fall of an unpopular pro-Soviet regime and bore a resemblance to the U.S. intervention in Vietnam (see pages 58–67), also designed to preserve a friendly government that was on the point of collapse.

The United States regarded Latin America as its own turf and supported pro-American regimes with arms, money, and training to combat rebel groups. It also intervened, directly or indirectly, to achieve the overthrow of governments considered too left-wing—as in Guatemala in 1954, Chile in 1973, and Grenada in 1983. Throughout the 1980s the United States government organized, armed, and trained guerrillas in a campaign to bring down the left-wing government in Nicaragua.

Ending the Cold War

The United States was also involved in the promotion of guerrilla warfare in Afghanistan in the 1980s, arming and training local Muslim guerrillas fighting the Soviet army. The humiliation of Soviet forces in Afghanistan, which were forced to withdraw in 1989, was undoubtedly one of the factors leading to the eventual collapse of Soviet power. Another was the strain of ever-increasing defense spending as the relatively poor Soviet Union sought to maintain nuclear equality with the economically more powerful United States.

The sudden collapse of Soviet power, and then of the Soviet Union itself, between 1987 and 1991 was in no sense chiefly a military event, and certainly not a conflict won on the Cold War battlefield. The 40-year-old Cold War, a conflict that had cost huge amounts of money—and cost a large number of lives across the globe—ended because one of the two superpowers, the Soviet Union, lost both the political will to sustain a battle for world supremacy and the financial ability to compete with the much richer United States.

Troops of the U.S. 82nd Airborne Division pictured during their operation against the Caribbean island of Grenada, October 1983. The U.S. government was concerned about Soviet-backed Cuban involvement in the island's affairs and, under the pretext of protecting local and U.S. lives, invaded.

THE THREAT OF TERRORISM

Since 1945 many political groups have adopted the terrorist tactics of bombing, kidnapping, hijacking, and assassination to achieve their ends. Some terrorists have had precise and limited goals, while others have embraced terrorism as a general technique for destabilizing society and creating the conditions for a supposed world revolution. Some states have backed terrorism as a form of undeclared warfare against their enemies. Countries threatened by terrorism have formed their own elite units to combat the danger.

The bloodiest terrorist campaign of the period immediately after World War II was that waged by the Jews in Palestine against the British government, which controlled the territory, and the local Palestinian Arabs. The Jewish community was trying to create an independent state. The worst outrage was the bombing of the British administrative headquarters in Jerusalem, the King David Hotel, by the Jewish terrorist group Irgun in July 1946. The bomb killed 91 people, many of them civilians. The Irgun had, in fact, telephoned a warning about the bomb, but it was ignored by British officials at the hotel. The British also faced other terrorist campaigns by groups seeking independence, notably in Cyprus (1955–58) and in Aden (1963–67).

Rescue workers carry away the injured from the ruins of the King David Hotel in Jerusalem after the bomb attack by the Jewish organization Irgun, July 1946.

International terrorism

France's colonial wars, especially that in Algeria in North Africa (see pages 20–23), also involved terrorist attacks. Both the native Algerian Muslims, seeking independence from France, and the white settlers dedicated to keeping Algeria French carried out terrorist campaigns in France, planting bombs and committing murders on the streets of Paris, the capital. The white Algerians narrowly failed in an attempt to assassinate the French president, Charles de Gaulle, in 1963.

It was only in the late 1960s, however, that terrorism became an international activity and a threat to world stability. The

rise of international terrorism was the result of two simultaneous developments: the growth of Palestinian Arab groups dedicated to the overthrow of the Jewish state of Israel, and the spread of extreme left-wing ideas among certain groups in Europe.

Palestinian terrorism

Al Fatah, the Palestinian group led by Yassir Arafat, began raids on Israel in 1964. However, it was the Popular Front for the Liberation of Palestine (PFLP) that from 1968 began to attack targets outside Israel to publicize the Palestinian cause. The attacks were aimed chiefly at El Al, the Israeli airline, but soon spread more widely. The PFLP saw the struggle as part of a worldwide revolution, and made the moderate Arab states, the United States, and Western nations generally its targets.

The classic operation of this phase of terrorist activity was the "skyjack." In the absence of strict security measures at airports, terrorists found it easy to board aircraft while carrying arms and hijack them, forcing the pilot to fly to an airport they regarded as safe. Once there they would hold the aircraft and passengers hostage, making demands—usually for the release of other terrorists captured in earlier operations.

The climax of the PFLP's campaign came in a spectacular flurry of air hijacks in September 1970. Palestinians seized no less than four airliners—two American, one British, and one Swiss—and just failed to seize an Israeli jet in the Netherlands. Three of the airliners were flown to Dawson's Field in Jordan, where they were eventually blown up in front of the world's television cameras. The immediate response to the hijacking was an attack on

One of the airliners hijacked by members of the Popular Front for the Liberation of Palestine and flown to Dawson's Field in Jordan is destroyed by a bomb, September 1970. The hijack marked the beginning of the international terrorist campaign.

CARLOS THE JACKAL

Ilich Ramirez Sanchez, known as "Carlos" or "the Jackal," was the son of a family of wealthy Venezuelan Communists. He grew up with a taste for high living, but also a devotion to extreme left-wing ideas. In the early 1970s he was drawn into the internationalist terrorist network based on the Popular Front for the Liberation of Palestine.

From 1973 onward he was involved in a series of terrorist acts, allegedly including missile attacks on El Al airliners taking off from Orly airport, Paris, in January 1975. The most spectacular of his actions, and the one that made him famous, was the kidnapping of 11 senior oil ministers in Vienna, Austria, in December 1975.

The decline of international terrorism toward the end of the 1970s made Carlos seem an outdated figure. In August 1994 he was arrested in Sudan, East Africa, and handed over to the French. He was convicted of committing multiple murders.

armed Palestinian groups by Jordan's King Hussein's armed forces, which drove the Palestinians out of the country, forcing them to relocate in Lebanon and Syria.

The PFLP's view that the Palestinian struggle was part of a world revolutionary struggle made it natural for them to establish links with left-wing terrorist groups that were forming in Europe at the end of the 1960s. These groups were of two distinct kinds. One type consisted of students or middle-class intellectuals, such as the notorious "Carlos the Jackal" (Ilich Ramirez Sanchez), who had become disillusioned with peaceful politics after the failure of the students' and workers' movements that had rocked Western Europe in 1968. They decided to turn to an armed struggle. The most notable examples were the Red Army Faction in West Germany, also known as the Baader–Meinhof gang, and the Red Brigades in Italy.

Terror's international links

The other type of European terrorist movement was essentially nationalist, and had more in common with the Israeli or Greek Cypriot terrorist organizations of the 1940s and 1950s. They were trying to break away from the country of which they were a part. The prime examples were the Irish Republican Army (IRA, at the time known as the Provisional IRA) in Northern Ireland, and the Basque separatist movement in Spain. Both engaged in terrorist campaigns on a considerable scale in the 1970s.

It was a terrorist group from Asia, however, that first revealed to the world the extent of Palestinian international contacts. On May 30, 1972, three members of the Japanese Red Army were among passengers who disembarked from an airliner at Lod airport near Tel Aviv, Israel. Firing indiscriminately and throwing hand grenades inside the airport building, they killed 26 people and injured a further 76.

It was not the PFLP but another Palestinian group under Arafat's direction, Black September, that was responsible for the most notorious incident of the whole period, the attack on Israeli athletes during the 1972 Olympic Games in Munich, then in West Germany. Eight terrorists entered the Olympic village and broke into the building where the Israelis were housed, killing two, and taking nine hostages. German negotiators agreed to provide an airliner to fly the terrorists and their hostages to Tunisia. At the airport, however, police marksmen attempted to gun down the terrorists. After a prolonged firefight, all the hostages were killed before the last terrorists were captured.

New terror groups

By 1973 the Palestinian cause had been thoroughly brought to the attention of the world. The main Palestinian leaders, including Arafat, decided to end the international terror campaign, which they now saw as tending to hurt rather than further their cause. But there were plenty of smaller Palestinian groups prepared to carry on the terrorist tradition. The government of Iraq backed terror chief Abu Nidal, who masterminded a string of attacks, especially on Palestinians who favored some agreement with Israel. The Libyan leader Muammar Gadhafi set up his own

A bomb placed by the Provisional Irish Republican Army explodes inside a hotel in Ballycastle, Northern Ireland, 1979. Remarkably, injuries were slight and no one was killed in the attack. The IRA, a nationalist group, conducted a terror campaign to unite British-controlled Northern Ireland with the Irish Republic.

terrorist movement, National Arab Youth for the Liberation of Palestine (NAYLP). The PFLP's international network was inherited by Wadi Haddad, head of the movement's overseas operations, who continued his campaign independently.

The authorities fight back

Haddad's terror campaign from 1973 to 1978 depended heavily on his links with the German Red Army Faction and with the Venezuelan Carlos the Jackal, who masterminded European operations. Baader–Meinhof terrorists took part in the Carlos-led kidnapping of the world's leading oil ministers in Vienna, Austria, in December 1975—an operation intended to punish wealthy pro-Western Middle East states for their failure to back the Palestinians. German terrorists also took part in the Entebbe, Uganda, hijacking in 1976, which was ended successfully by an Israeli antiterrorist squad. The Israelis had become involved because many of the passengers on board were Jewish.

The success at Entebbe, in which most of the hostages were rescued, showed that the world was becoming a less easy place for terrorists. Governments across the world had been ill-prepared to meet the upsurge of international terrorism. But from the early 1970s, they began to organize antiterrorist squads, coordinate intelligence, and put up resistance to terrorists. Specialist units such as Britain's SAS (Special Air Service), the German Grenzshutzgruppe (GSG9— Border Action Group 9), and the U.S. Delta Force were trained in antiterrorism.

The turning point in the fight against international terrorism came in October 1977. Baader–Meinhof took hostage a West German businessman, Hanns-Martin Schleyer, and demanded the release of all their members held in German prisons— including most of the movement's leadership. At the same time, a Lufthansa airliner was hijacked by Palestinian terrorists to support the Red Army Faction's demand.

A German antiterrorist squad , aided by two SAS men, pursued the hijacked airliner to Mogadishu, Somalia. They stormed the aircraft and freed the hostages, killing

Members of West Germany's top anti-terrorist squad return home after their successful hostage-rescue mission to Mogadishu, Somalia, in 1977.

THE IRANIAN EMBASSY SIEGE

On April 30, 1980, five Arab gunmen took over the Iranian Embassy in Knightsbridge, London, taking 20 people hostage. They were demanding the release of 91 Arabs being held as political prisoners in Iran. British antiterrorist forces put the embassy under siege. After six days, on May 5, the gunmen shot one of their hostages and threatened to shoot more.

In response, members of the British elite Special Air Service (SAS) antiterrorist unit stormed the building. SAS men on the balconies at the front of the embassy used an explosive charge to blow in a window and hurled in stun grenades, which exploded with a deafening noise and bright light, thereby stunning anyone in range. Others used ropes to drop down from the roof at the back of the building and broke in through windows at the rear.

As the SAS entered the building, the gunmen opened fire, killing one of their hostages and severely wounding another. The SAS teams shot four of the gunmen dead in a brief firefight but a fifth was saved when he sheltered among the hostages, making it impossible for the SAS to shoot him. The embassy was gutted by fires started by the explosions of the SAS's stun grenades.

Members of Britain's Special Air Service, the country's top antiterrorist unit, prepare to storm the Iranian Embassy in London to rescue hostages held by Arab terrorists, May 1980.

The remains of the Alfred P. Murrah building in Oklahoma City after it was destroyed by a bomb planted by a right-wing opponent of the U.S. government in April 1995.

or capturing all the terrorists. In the aftermath of this operation, the Red Army Faction leaders in prison all died, allegedly by suicide. However, Schleyer was also killed by his captors.

This bloodbath marked the end of the greatest period of international terrorism. Lacking any roots in West German society, the Red Army Faction had almost faded away by the end of the 1970s. The Italian Red Brigades also proved short-lived. From 1974 these young former students carried out a series of terrorist actions that culminated in the kidnapping and murder of Italian political leader Aldo Moro in 1978. But their apparent strength was an illusion, for like their German equivalent they lacked any substantial base of popular support and soon disappeared in the face of a determined police crackdown.

Europe's longest terror campaigns

The Provisional Irish Republican Army (IRA) and Basque movements were far more durable because they had deep roots in minorities hostile to the government—Catholics in Northern Ireland and Basques in Spain. The IRA sustained a terrorist campaign against the British both in Northern Ireland and on the British mainland for 27 years, from 1970 to 1997, with a few cease-fires. The Basques began their campaign against the Spanish government and authorities in 1967 but agreed to a cease-fire in 1998. The Basque situation is open to a political solution that might end the violence. Both campaigns showed how terrorists make it difficult to achieve a political settlement.

Terrorist activity was by no means confined to left-wing groups or radical nationalists. In Italy, extreme right-wing terrorists took far more lives than the Red Brigades did—killing 80 people, for example, in a single bombing at Bologna railway station in 1980. In Northern Ireland, Protestant groups determined to preserve the existing political system matched the IRA in murders. And in the United States, the bombing of the Alfred P. Murrah building in Oklahoma City in April 1995, in which 168 people died, was the work of right-wing extremists hostile to the U.S. government and its agencies.

In the 1980s and 1990s, however, the Middle East remained the center of world terrorism. A revolution in Iran in 1979 overthrew the pro-Western king and replaced him with an Islamic fundamentalist regime, one based on the teachings of the Muslim holy book, the Koran, headed by the Ayatollah Khomeini, a Muslim religious leader. Iran, deeply anti-Western, immediately became a focus for violent agitation against the United States. In November 1979, for example, Iranian students took over the U.S. embassy in Teheran, the Iranian capital, taking 90 hostages, mainly U.S. citizens. The U.S. antiterrorist unit Delta Force tried to rescue the hostages in April 1980, but the operation failed. The hostages were finally freed in Janaury 1981.

The terror continues

The list of terrorist outrages is continually added to. Prominent incidents included the blowing up of a Pan American Jumbo jet over Lockerbie, Scotland, in December 1988, killing 270 people. Although a Palestinian state has been created by agreement between the PLO and Israel, Israel remained the target of a terrorist campaign in the mid-1990s. Despite the use of large resources to counter terrorism, it remains a threat to peace.

The cockpit of the Jumbo jet blown up while flying over Lockerbie, southern Scotland, in December 1988. Those believed to have carried out the attack have not yet been brought to trial, although negotiations are continuing between Britain and Libya, whose nationals are thought to have planted the bomb.

THE WAR
IN VIETNAM

In 1955, after the French withdrawal from Indochina (see pages 10–13), the Republic of South Vietnam was founded with Ngo Dinh Diem as its president. From the outset the United States backed South Vietnam as a barrier to the spread of Communism in the region, as represented by Ho Chi Minh's North Vietnam. But Diem's rule was corrupt and oppressive. He was a Roman Catholic and discriminated against South Vietnamese Buddhists. In the rural areas Diem's regime was extremely unpopular.

U.S. military advisers on patrol with troops of the South Vietnamese army. U.S. involvement in the country rose from a few hundred men in the early 1960s to over 620,000 in 1969, the peak year of U.S. commitment to the war in Vietnam.

In 1959 South Vietnamese Communist guerrillas of the National Liberation Front (NLF), popularly known as the Viet Cong, began a campaign to overthrow Diem. Backed by North Vietnam, the NLF uprising rapidly spread through much of rural South Vietnam. Many of the Viet Cong's weapons and supplies came down the Ho Chi Minh Trail, which stretched from North Vietnam, through Laos and Cambodia, into South Vietnam. In 1961 the United States, which was already training the South Vietnamese army (ARVN—Army of the Republic of Vietnam), started sending military advisers and helicopter pilots into action.

The U.S. government was deeply worried about the situation in Southeast Asia. Laos, another of the countries of former French Indochina, was in the grip of a complex civil war and could be an easy subject to a Communist takeover. Basing their policies on the "domino theory"—that the fall of one pro-American regime in Southeast Asia might lead to the fall of others—U.S. administrations were sucked into stopping the spread of Communist power in South Vietnam at almost any cost.

U.S. forces arrive

In 1963 the United States backed a South Vietnamese coup against Diem, because they thought he was too bad a ruler to resist the Communists. Diem was killed. But this only plunged South Vietnam into political instability and bound the U.S.

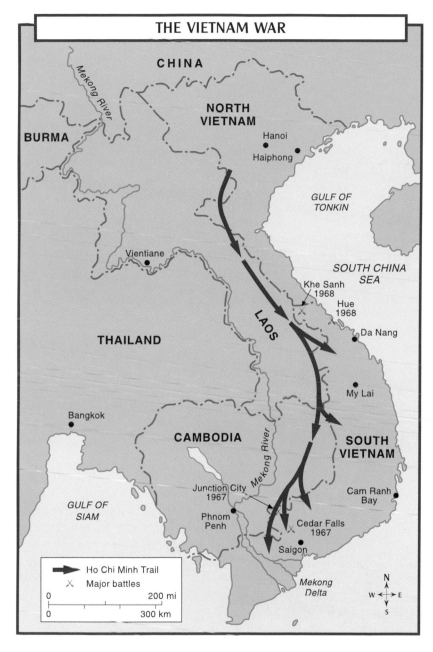

THE VIETNAM WAR

CHINA

BURMA

NORTH VIETNAM

Hanoi

Haiphong

GULF OF TONKIN

Vientiane

SOUTH CHINA SEA

Khe Sanh 1968

Hue 1968

LAOS

THAILAND

Da Nang

My Lai

Bangkok

CAMBODIA

Mekong River

SOUTH VIETNAM

Junction City 1967

GULF OF SIAM

Phnom Penh

Cam Ranh Bay

Cedar Falls 1967

Saigon

Mekong Delta

➤ Ho Chi Minh Trail
✕ Major battles

| 0 | 200 mi |
| 0 | 300 km |

N
W ← → E
S

The United States was involved in the Vietnam War from 1965 to 1975. For much of this period the U.S. troops in South Vietnam had to fight against the Viet Cong, a guerrilla force. Although the U.S. military was able to inflict heavy casualties on the guerrillas, it was never able to deliver a decisive defeat on them. As American casualties grew, U.S. commitment to the war fell away. In 1975 the Viet Cong, aided by regulars from North Vietnam, overthrew the South's government and united the country.

ever closer to that country. Meanwhile, the guerrilla movement continued to progress, outmatching the government forces in commitment, popular support, and fighting skills. By 1964 it seemed only a matter of time before Saigon (now Ho Chi Minh City), the South Vietnamese capital, fell to the NLF.

A North Vietnamese antiaircraft crew sweeps the skies for signs of U.S. aircraft during Operation Rolling Thunder, a bombing campaign designed to persuade North Vietnam to halt its support for the Viet Cong guerrillas in South Vietnam.

U.S. Secretary of Defense Robert McNamara, along with other U.S. political and military leaders, felt that the key to the military situation lay in North Vietnam. However, the desire to keep the conflict limited and avoid a war with one of the major Communist powers (Russia or China) ruled out an invasion of the North. The Americans decided to increase pressure on North Vietnam, to persuade its leaders to call off the war in the South.

Growing U.S. involvement

In August 1964, U.S. harassment of North Vietnam led to the Gulf of Tonkin incident, when a U.S. destroyer, USS *Maddox*, sailing just off the North Vietnamese coast, was attacked by North Vietnamese vessels. A similar incident was reported but unconfirmed two days later. Whatever the truth of this shadowy incident, it provided a pretext for U.S. bombing raids on North Vietnam and for the passage of a resolution by Congress that effectively gave the president, Lyndon B. Johnson, a free hand to increase U.S. involvement in Vietnam.

In February 1965, the United States began the systematic bombing of North Vietnam, a campaign known as Operation Rolling Thunder. In the same month U.S. Marines landed at Da Nang in South Vietnam, the first U.S. ground combat units committed to the war. By the end of the year, 181,000 U.S. troops were operating in South Vietnam. Commanded by General

William C. Westmoreland, they took over most of the responsibility for fighting the Viet Cong from the poorly functioning South Vietnamese army.

The American soldiers' task was a difficult one. The Viet Cong, supported by increasing numbers of North Vietnamese Army (NVA) troops, effectively controlled about 70 percent of South Vietnam, including areas within 15 miles (24 km) of Saigon. Although lightly equipped, they were skilled in the guerrilla arts of concealment, ambush, and the use of booby traps.

Searching for victory

Westmoreland chose to use what he saw as his two great advantages over the Viet Cong: mobility and firepower. The use of fleets of helicopters would allow the American troops to move swiftly into the heart of Viet Cong territory and search out the enemy. When contact was established, American commanders would call in the massive destructive capacity of U.S. air power, artillery located at firebases (fortified camps), and naval guns to destroy guerrilla formations. The measure of success was the "body count"—the figures for numbers of Communists killed that were regularly published by the Americans.

As the U.S. poured ever larger numbers of troops into South Vietnam, rising to over 480,000 by the end of 1967, they undoubtedly succeeded in stemming the tide of the guerrilla campaign. Major operations, such as Cedar Falls in January 1967 and Junction City in February through May of the same year, at least temporarily won back areas of the country long held by the Viet Cong. American soldiers fought with courage and commitment in difficult conditions.

But the problem for the Americans was that, whatever military successes they scored, they seemed no nearer a decisive victory. The bombing of North Vietnam only strengthened the resolution of the North Vietnamese to fight on. The supply route from North Vietnam to the fighters in the South, the Ho Chi Minh Trail, continued to function, despite large-scale U.S. air attacks on both the route and convoys traveling down it.

Meanwhile, the scale of American losses in the war was beginning to trouble the U.S. public—9,378 Americans died in Vietnam in 1967. A growing minority in the United States was troubled by the war itself. It was difficult to distinguish between guerrillas and peasants in South Vietnam, and U.S. forces did not always trouble to make the distinction. American military action

FIREBASES

Fire support bases were an essential element in American plans for fighting the Vietnam War. Placed in areas where contact with guerrillas was expected, they were intended to give artillery cover to infantry patrols and to contribute to the "body count" by inflicting heavy losses on enemy units drawn into attacking them.

At the heart of the average firebase was a helicopter landing zone. A circle of mines and barbed wire formed the boundary of the base. Inside this, a ring of foxholes commanded a clear field of fire. The battery of artillery in a firebase normally consisted of about half a dozen 105 mm or 155 mm howitzers.

If the firebase came under attack, its commander could call in an astonishing array of aircraft to provide support, including helicopter gunships, cargo planes fitted out as fixed-wing gun platforms, ground-attack aircraft, and even B-52 bombers. Very few U.S. firebases were ever overrun during the Vietnam War.

A helicopter flies in supplies during the building of a U.S. firebase. The smoke was used to direct its pilot to the correct location.

led to the destruction of villages, the destruction of crops, and the incidental killing or maiming of civilians. Critics pointed out that these things were being done to the South Vietnamese—the people the Americans had been sent to protect.

The critical moment of the American war in Vietnam came in early 1968. On January 31 Viet Cong guerrillas and North Vietnamese troops attacked more than 100 cities and towns the length and breadth of South Vietnam. This Tet Offensive (named after the Vietnamese holiday on which it started) was a clear military failure. Counterattacks by American and ARVN forces won back all the towns or districts that had been seized in the initial attacks, inflicting heavy losses from which the Viet Cong never fully recovered.

However, the Tet Offensive delivered a profound shock to the American public, who were astonished to see guerrillas attempting to take over the U.S. Embassy in Saigon after three years of efforts to suppress them. It made both the American public and U.S. leaders doubt that the war in Vietnam could be won.

In March 1968, President Johnson turned down General Westmoreland's request for yet more troops to fight in Vietnam, and to extend operations into Laos and Cambodia. Instead, the president scaled down the bombing of North Vietnam as a first move toward negotiations with the Communists. Preliminary talks began the following month. Actual peace talks began in Paris, the French capital, in May, but the war continued.

Faltering U.S. resolve

Between the spring of 1968 and the autumn of 1969, as the war in South Vietnam continued with unabated ferocity, American firepower gradually had an impact. The fighting was increasingly concentrated in more remote regions of the country, away from Saigon and the other coastal cities. Meanwhile, the Phoenix Program run by the U.S. Central Intelligence Agency (CIA) targeted the Communists' underground network operating in government-controlled areas, identifying and then eliminating leading Communists and sympathizers.

But the Americans' will to fight had been fatally weakened. In June 1968 Westmoreland was replaced as U.S. commander by General Creighton W. Abrams. Abrams vigorously pursued a policy of Vietnamization—making the ARVN gradually replace U.S. troops in the front line of the war. Against a background of mounting antiwar protests and adverse media coverage of the war, Richard M. Nixon was elected president in November 1968. Although strongly anti-Communist, Nixon was committed to bringing the U.S. troops in Vietnam home. The U.S. public would no longer stand for the huge numbers of American casualties. Also, by 1969 the U.S. Army in Vietnam was becoming demoralized, with a high level of drug abuse and antiwar sentiment increasing in the ranks.

U.S. forces open fire on a suspected Viet Cong position. The chief problem for the U.S. military in the Vietnam War was to bring the Viet Cong to battle. The guerrillas would often retreat from the battlefield if they were in any danger of being defeated, thereby giving themselves the chance to fight again later on more favorable terms.

While beginning U.S. troop withdrawals in 1969, Nixon also widened the war to attack North Vietnamese bases in Cambodia. He authorized bombing raids on Cambodia and armed raids into both Cambodia and Laos. The Americans also backed the overthrow of Cambodia's ruler, Prince Noradom Sihanouk, by an army officer, Marshal Lon Nol. The upshot of these actions was to make the government of Cambodia unstable and to cause an increase in activity by the Cambodian Communist guerrilla movement, the Khmer Rouge.

Victory for the North

In March 1972, the nature of the fighting in Vietnam fundamentally altered. With American ground troops rapidly shipping home and no longer directly engaged in a ground combat role, the North Vietnamese leadership decided to invade South Vietnam. The attacks by the NVA were soon halted due to a combination of U.S. air power and unexpectedly stiff resistance from the ARVN, but a cease-fire in October left the North Vietnamese in control of key border areas in the north and west of South Vietnam.

After a final display of American power in the second half of December 1972, when B-52 bombers devastated targets in the Northern cities of Haiphong and Hanoi, the U.S. signed a peace agreement with the North Vietnamese and the NLF on January 23, 1973. By the time of the peace treaty, over 46,000 U.S. troops had died in action in Vietnam.

Where the NVA and the ARVN confronted one another, occasional small-scale fighting continued throughout 1973 and 1974. The North Vietnamese methodically built up their supplies and equipment for a renewed offensive. Meanwhile, South Vietnam

WAR AND THE MEDIA

The Vietnam War has been called "the first television war." Daily TV news reports brought the war into American homes with a vividness unmatched by earlier media. Although briefed and directed by military press officers, TV and print journalists were mostly able to cover the war freely. They often filed stories that painted a gloomy view of the military situation, especially during the Tet Offensive of 1968. Journalists also highlighted the suffering of civilians in the war, thus promoting antiwar sentiment. The most notable case was the massacre of South Vietnamese civilians by U.S. troops at the village of My Lai in March 1968.

Some U.S. military leaders felt that, in effect, the press lost the war in Vietnam by undermining morale at home, when the army was on the point of winning in the field. Since Vietnam, U.S. armed forces have been determined to control news coverage in time of war. However, it seems clear that it was in fact the nature of the Vietnam War, its heavy casualties and lack of decisive victories or clearly understood aims, which undermined public support.

U.S. troops are interviewed by an army reporter after returning from a mission.

was still almost totally dependent on the United States for money, supplies, and equipment. When Congress cut off military aid in 1974, South Vietnam was doomed.

The end came with startling speed. A series of NVA advances began in December 1974. By March 1975, it had become clear that the ARVN was falling apart. The United States refused to intervene to save its former ally. On April 30, amid chaotic scenes in Saigon as Americans and favored South Vietnamese officials

HELICOPTER GUNSHIPS

At the start of their involvement in Vietnam, the Americans did not have a helicopter gunship. They managed by fitting out troop-carrying helicopters with an array of machine guns, grenade-launchers, and rockets to fill the role of a gunship. In 1967, however, the AH-1G Huey Cobra helicopter arrived on the battlefield. Crewed by a gunner and a pilot, with the gunner sitting in front, the Cobra was an extremely efficient and formidable attack helicopter.

In Vietnam, it was most often armed with a machine gun and a grenade-launcher beneath the nose, plus air-to-ground rockets and additional machine guns or cannon beneath its small wings.

The helicopter's rockets were an especially impressive aerial artillery weapon, capable of delivering a barrage comparable to that from a single howitzer. After the Vietnam War the Cobra gunship was adapted to perform the role of an antitank helicopter.

U.S. troops leap from a hovering transport heli-copter. This particular version has been fitted with machine guns to protect the soldiers from enemy fire.

Regular North Vietnamese troops storm through Tan Son Nhut, Saigon's chief airbase, at the end of their offensive in 1975, which saw the defeat of the South Vietnamese.

fled by helicopter, North Vietnamese tanks rolled into Saigon. While South Vietnam was falling to the Communists, so too were neighboring Laos and Cambodia.

The war had had a devastating effect on Vietnam, which was officially united in June 1976. Millions of peasants had been killed, wounded, or driven from their homes. A third of the land in the South was poisoned with chemical sprays or had been laid waste by bombs and shells.

The fighting continues

The Communist takeovers did not bring an end to suffering or an end to the fighting. The Khmer Rouge regime, installed in the Cambodian capital, Phnom Penh, in 1975, immediately proved itself more extreme and brutal than anyone had believed possible, driving the population of the city into the country to become slave laborers. In Vietnam itself life was hard, both through the effects of the war and poor management of the economy.

In December 1978 the Vietnamese invaded Cambodia in force and drove out the Khmer Rouge government. China, which backed the Khmer Rouge, invaded Vietnam in a brief border war the following year. The Khmer Rouge continued to fight a brutal guerrilla war against the Vietnamese until Vietnam withdrew its troops in 1989. The occasional outbreaks of fighting and the complex political conflicts continued in Cambodia throughout the 1990s.

WARS IN THE PERSIAN GULF

The Persian Gulf (also known as the Arabian Gulf) became an area of immense economic and strategic significance in the post-1945 period, because it was the source of much of the oil consumed by Western nations. It was also an area of great instability. In 1979 the leader of Iran was overthrown and a radical Muslim regime headed by a religious leader, Ayatollah Khomeini, gained power. Also in 1979, Saddam Hussein took over as leader of the military regime in Iraq. Enmity between Iraq and Iran now became intense.

After increasing border clashes Saddam launched a major invasion of southern Iran on September 22, 1980. The following month the Iraqis captured the city of Khorramshahr, but they failed to seize the crucial port and refinery city of Abadan. Iraq's armed forces were superior in tanks, artillery, and aircraft to the Iranians. But the Iranians were inspired by religious and patriotic zeal and fought back with an almost total disregard for the human cost. The Iranian Revolutionary Guards, consisting of those Iranians most loyal to Khomeini, led human-wave attacks on Iraqi positions, driving Saddam's forces back across the border.

The Iranian religious leader Ayatollah Khomeini took over as leader of his country in 1979. Iran was soon plunged into a long and vicious war with its neighbor Iraq, which remains ruled by the dictator Saddam Hussein.

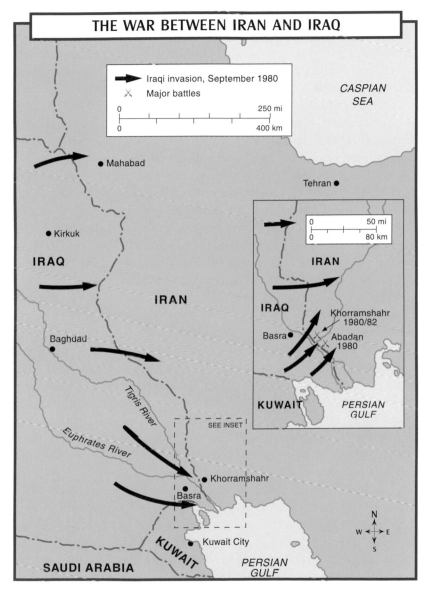

THE WAR BETWEEN IRAN AND IRAQ

→ Iraqi invasion, September 1980
✗ Major battles

0   250 mi
0   400 km

CASPIAN SEA

Mahabad

Tehran

Kirkuk

IRAQ

IRAN

0   50 mi
0   80 km

IRAN

IRAQ

Khorramshahr 1980/82
Basra
Abadan 1980

Baghdad

Tigris River

Euphrates River

KUWAIT

PERSIAN GULF

SEE INSET

Khorramshahr

Basra

KUWAIT

Kuwait City

N
W ← → E
S

SAUDI ARABIA

PERSIAN GULF

The war between Iran and Iraq lasted from September 1980 until August 1988. The Iraqis began the war by invading Iran, but their attacks soon bogged down. Neither side was able to inflict a decisive defeat on the other, and the troops dug in, creating deep lines of trenches and fortifications. Any attacks that were made usually led to huge numbers of casualties with little or no gain.

The conflict quickly became stalemated, with neither side able to win a decisive victory. Neither side showed much imagination or flexibility, the Iraqis using their firepower to inflict heavy losses on the Iranians, while the Iranians relied on sheer weight of numbers. Losses, particularly Iranian, were very heavy. Iraq extended the war into the Persian Gulf itself by attacking Iranian shipping. Both sides carried out long-range missile attacks on one another's cities, but with very limited effect. By 1988, as Iran seemed to be getting the upper hand on the land battlefield, Saddam took the decision to use chemical weapons (bombs or shells filled with poisons). It was the last act of a conflict that neither seemed able to win. A cease-fire was agreed on in August, ending a war that had killed at least a million people.

During the Iraq–Iran War the Western powers and Arab states, such as Saudi Arabia, had backed Iraq, fearing that Iran's Islamic revolution would spread. But Saddam soon revealed himself as an even greater threat to peace and stability in the Middle East than the religious leaders in Teheran, the Iranian capital. The war with Iran had left Iraq saddled with huge debts. Its ability to pay off these debts was threatened by falling oil prices, caused in part by the failure of other Arab countries, including Kuwait, one of the leading oil-producing countries in the Middle East, to stick to agreed production quotas. In July 1990, Iraq began to increase its pressure on Kuwait by reopening a territorial dispute.

Iraq invades Kuwait

Iraqi armored columns invaded Kuwait on August 2, brushing aside the minimal resistance they met. In less than 24 hours the country was under Iraqi control. The UN responded by imposing tough economic sanctions on Iraq, which prevent Iraq and other countries from trading with each other. The United States and Britain sent aircraft to Saudi Arabia, where they were soon joined by troops from the United States and from some Arab countries. These land-based forces were backed by powerful U.S. carrier fleets in the Persian Gulf.

The initial deployment of the forces to block Saddam, called Operation Desert Shield, was designed to defend Saudi Arabia and its vast oil reserves from a possible Iraqi attack. In November, however, the United States decided on a major addition to its forces in the region, increasing its troop levels in Saudi Arabia from 200,000 to 500,000 men. Britain and France also increased their commitment, and Egypt and Syria contributed substantial armored formations. Other countries also provided forces. Together they became known as the Coalition (anti-Iraqi forces).

On November 29, the United Nations set a deadline of January 15, 1991, for an Iraqi withdrawal from Kuwait. After that date the UN authorized the use of "all necessary means" to drive the Iraqis out. General Norman Schwarzkopf, the U.S. commander of the Coalition forces in the Gulf, knew that his ground forces were outnumbered by about two to one by the

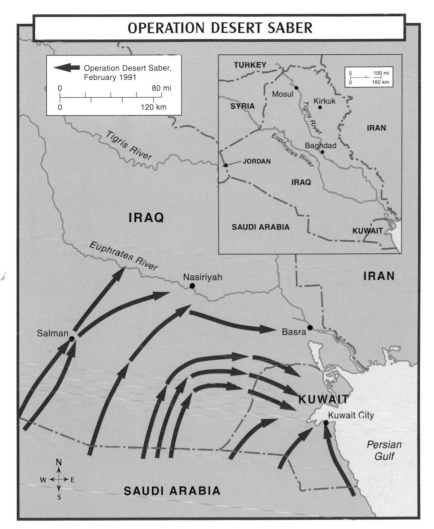

OPERATION DESERT SABER

Operation Desert Saber, February 1991

0 ——————— 80 mi
0 ——————— 120 km

TURKEY

Mosul

Kirkuk

SYRIA

Tigris River

Euphrates River

Baghdad

JORDAN

IRAN

IRAQ

SAUDI ARABIA

KUWAIT

0 ——— 100 mi
0 ——— 160 km

Tigris River

IRAQ

Euphrates River

Nasiriyah

Salman

Basra

IRAN

KUWAIT

Kuwait City

Persian Gulf

N
W — E
S

SAUDI ARABIA

Operation Desert Saber was the ground offensive that was launched against the Iraqi forces occupying Kuwait on February 23, 1991. The Iraqis were expected to fight hard to hold on to Kuwait, but were in fact smashed in just four days.

Iraqis, who were dug into defensive positions and heavily equipped with tanks and artillery. With Coalition air power in the Gulf having risen to almost 2,000 aircraft, an air offensive was the obvious way to open the campaign. Operation Desert Storm, the air offensive against Iraq, was launched on the night of January 16–17 with a devastating series of coordinated air strikes that established complete air superiority in hours.

Over the weeks that followed, aircraft and missiles systematically destroyed Iraq's military command and communications systems, as well as inflicting immense physical and psychological damage on the Iraqi forces massed in Kuwait. Iraq retaliated with medium-range missile attacks on Israel and Saudi Arabia, but

STEALTH

Stealth is the term used to describe various technologies that make it difficult for an enemy to identify an aircraft on radar. The United States was the first country to develop and deploy stealth aircraft. These were the F-117 Blackhawk and the B-2 bomber. The Blackhawk first saw service in the invasion of Panama in December 1989, but was deployed in much greater numbers during the 1991 Persian Gulf War.

Much of stealth technology remains top secret, but two of its components have been documented. The F-117, for example, has a very angular shape. This means that radar waves bounce off it at odd angles, and most are not reflected back to enemy radar stations. Second, the aircraft is coated in a radar-absorbing material, which again reduces the intensity of radar waves being bounced back. Consequently, it is very difficult for enemy radar to get a fix on a stealth aircraft.

F-117s led the way in the Coalition's air offensive against Iraq in 1991. They were able to penetrated Iraq's defenses and pound key targets. Despite flying into the heart of enemy territory, the F-117 suffered no combat losses during the war to liberate Kuwait.

An F-117 Blackhawk returns to its base in Saudi Arabia after a raid against Iraq. The parachute helps slow the landing speed.

fears that the Iraqis might use their chemical warheads proved unfounded. About 80 Iraqi missiles were fired during the war, most against Israel. but the worst damage they inflicted was through a chance hit on a U.S. barracks in Dharhan, Saudi Arabia, which killed 27 Marines.

Coalition victory

After more than a month of "softening up," Operation Desert Saber, the ground offensive to liberate Kuwait, was launched on February 24. The bulk of the Coalition forces launched a massive attack that was designed to cut off the Iraqi troops in Kuwait. Armored forces powered across the border with Iraq. Some pushed north toward Baghdad, the Iraqi capital, while the U.S. Seventh Corps and the British First Armoured Division swung eastward to cross Kuwait's western border and engage Iraq's elite Republican Guard. U.S. Marines and other Coalition forces over-ran Iraqi trenches in southern Kuwait.

Almost as soon as the fighting began, it became clear that fears of heavy Coalition losses had been grossly exaggerated. The Iraqis had been utterly demoralized by the long bombardment they had suffered from air and land. The Coalition's superiority was overwhelming. They had complete command of the air, and had used this power to destroy Iraqi resistance. On February 27, Kuwait City was taken by Coalition troops. Iraqi forces fleeing northward in disorder toward Basra were cut to pieces by Coalition air power.

The United States ordered a cease-fire on the morning of February 28, exactly 100 hours after Operation Desert Saber had begun. Although Kuwait had been liberated, Saddam remained in control of Iraq. Coalition casualties were light—192 killed, about a quarter of those by "friendly fire" (casualties accidentally caused to one's own troops). Iraqi military losses cannot be calculated, but were probably around 50,000 dead.

One of the British First Armoured Division's Challenger tanks pushes through the desert to the west of Kuwait City in the final hours of the operation to liberate the country from the Iraqi invaders.

CONFLICT IN THE FUTURE

Although the ending of the Cold War in the late 1980s made the world a safer place for many, the ending of the rivalry between the United States and the Soviet Union has not led to any significant reduction in the number of wars being fought globally. Most of these are between neighboring countries or within an individual country. There are also likely to be more countries with stockpiles of nuclear weapons in the future, and some states may be willing to use them to settle disputes with their neighbors.

Although both the U.S. and the Soviet Union have made dramatic cuts in their numbers and types of nuclear weapons since the end of the Cold War in the late 1980s, other countries have been trying to develop nuclear missiles. For example, United Nations inspectors investigating Iraq's weapons program after the 1991 Persian Gulf War found a large program for developing nuclear warheads and the missiles needed to deliver them. Both India and Pakistan conducted a number of tests of nuclear devices in 1998 and North Korea has tested missiles able to carry nuclear weapons. These incidents suggest that the number of countries with nuclear weapons will increase in the future.

The moment of detonation of a nuclear bomb. Although both the United States and the Soviet Union agreed to cut their nuclear stockpiles at the end of the Cold War in the late 1980s, other countries are working hard to produce their own devices.

THE UNITED NATIONS

Dedicated to the "maintenance of international peace and security," the plan to found the United Nations was agreed upon between Britain, China, the Soviet Union, and the United States at a conference at Dumbarton Oaks, Washington D.C., in October 1944. The body itself came into force on October 24, 1945. The UN originally contained just 51 countries, but today contains over 180.

All members of the UN's General Assembly, the UN's debating chamber, are allowed up to five delegates and all have a single vote on any issue brought before the Assembly. The UN also has the Security Council. This consists of five permanent members–Britain, China, France, Russia, and the United States–and ten other member countries drawn from the wider UN membership who serve terms of two years. The Security Council is considered the main body for keeping international peace and security.

If war breaks out between members of the UN, the Security Council and, occasionally, the General Assembly can offer to negotiate between them, arrange a cease-fire, and provide forces to oversee it. UN peacekeeping forces, identified by their blue helmets, are allowed to fight only in self-defense and must be withdrawn if the host country makes such a request. The only time UN forces have actually been called upon to fight other than in self-defense was during the Korean War (1950–53). UN forces also provide humanitarian relief.

British troops, members of the UN peacekeeping force in Bosnia, 1990s.

Croatian troops open fire on Serbian troops in the town of Vukovar. The various states that were once part of Yugoslavia, including Croatia and Bosnia, have seen much violence and atrocities against civilians as peoples of different backgrounds have sought to either defend or take over territory that they believe should belong to them.

Although it is unlikely that the new or emerging nuclear countries would use them against the world's leading powers, it is quite possible that they could be used in localized, regional conflicts. Neighbors Pakistan and India, for example, have a long running dispute over a territory that both claim as their own, and have been to war twice in previous decades. Also there have been persistent rumors that the material for the manufacture of nuclear weapons has been spirited away from the former Soviet Union, most likely to countries eager to develop their own weapons.

Nuclear weapons have not been used in anger since World War II, and it remains unlikely that they will be used in the foreseeable future. However, wars using conventional, non-nuclear weapons are still common—and these weapons, despite their relative simplicity, are still capable of inflicting enormous casualties, great suffering, and massive destruction.

Wars in the future are likely to be between neighboring countries or within a single country. There are many reasons why these wars break out. Two countries might be political rivals, both eager to become the dominant power in the immediate area. They might be divided by ethnic or religious differences, or they might be economic rivals. Disputes over oil fields, minerals, and even water are likely to lead to war, if they cannot be resolved through negotiation.

Causes of wars

Wars within a country are often the result of ethnic or religious differences. One ethnic group, usually the minority, may feel discriminated against by the majority who hold power. They might be excluded from politics, receive poorer treatment, or be persecuted. Some groups wanted to break away from the state within which they live and set up their own country, or join up with a country in which people of their background are the majority.

The most obvious example of ethnic and religious warfare in recent times occurred in the former federal state of Yugoslavia, where various ethnic and religious groups, for example Serbs, Croatians, and Bosnians, and Christians and Muslims, fought each other to either create their own independent homelands or "purge" areas in which they were a majority or minority among other ethnic groups. The conflict gave the world a new phrase—"ethnic cleansing"—meaning the murder, torture, and forced expulsion of other ethnic groups.

Peace or war?

The world's leading powers have also been willing to intervene directly in other countries. Sometimes the intervention might be for humanitarian reasons, such as to aid civilians caught up in the fighting as was the case during the war in Yugoslavia, and during the civil war between rival warlords in Somalia, East Africa, in the early 1990s. Sometimes, however, these nations use military power for more complex reasons. The United States invaded the Caribbean island of Grenada in October 1983. The reasons given were to protect U.S. civilians and restore order after the murder of the island's leader. However, the U.S. was also concerned about Grenada's links with Cuba's Fidel Castro.

Wars will continue for the foreseeable future, and they are likely to be highly destructive, on a local scale at least. There seems less likelihood of a global confrontation, or a war that involves the use of nuclear weapons. It is to be hoped that agencies such as the United Nations will be able to prevent warfare, but as history shows, this has rarely been the case. It is likely that wars and terrorism will continue to inflict suffering on many peoples.

A member of the U.S. force sent to separate warring factions in Somalia, East Africa, stands guard over local villagers, December 1992.

GLOSSARY

arms control Attempts by governments and international organizations to control the spread and use of weapons, particularly nuclear warheads and the systems, such as rockets, needed to deliver them to a target.

arms race A situation in which two hostile countries invest huge amounts of time and money to build up their armed forces and equip them with the most powerful weapons available. In recent times the United States and Soviet Union took part in an arms race, each believing the other was winning.

conventional warfare A conflict in which those taking part use all the means at their disposal to win outright victory but stop short of using nuclear weapons.

deterrence The maintenance of one's own conventional and nuclear forces so strong and ready for immediate use that any country using its own conventional and nuclear forces would suffer an immediate and overwhelming counterattack. This balance of power is considered by some to have prevented a global conflict since World War II.

limited wars Conflicts in which one or both sides go into battle with a particular, usually short-term, objective. This aim is not usually the total military defeat of the enemy or the destruction of its country, rather it might be to retake a piece of land or punish an enemy for some aggressive action. The 1990 Persian Gulf War was a limited war in that the aim was to evict Iraqi troops from Kuwait, not to invade and conquer Iraq.

smart weapons A term used by the military to identify weapons, such as bombs and missiles, that have a high chance of hitting a target. Some, usually missiles, have an onboard computer that can be programmed to guide the weapon to its target once fired. Others include bombs, which can home in on a target that has been "illuminated" (identified) by a laser beam.

special forces Air, ground, and naval forces that, because of their special training, weapons, and equipment, are used to carry out difficult and dangerous operations thought to be beyond the abilities of ordinary soldiers. Such units may operate in small groups behind enemy lines or be trained in the techniques to deal with terrorist threats.

unconventional warfare Conflicts in which there are no large battles but frequent patrols, ambushes, and hit-and-run raids against usually stronger enemy forces. The aim of the forces waging this type of warfare is to wear the enemy down, undermining morale until it gives up the struggle.

BIBLIOGRAPHY

Note: *An asterisk (*) denotes a Young Adult title.*

*Brownstone, David and Franck, Irene. *Timelines of Warfare From 100,000 B.C. to the Present*. Little, Brown and Company, 1994

*Crenshaw, Martha and Pimlott, John (editors) *Encyclopedia of World Terrorism* (three volumes). M.E. Sharpe, Inc, 1997.

*Forty, George. *At War in Korea*. Sterling Publishing Co. Inc., 1997

*McCauley, Martin *The Origins of the Cold War, 1941–1949*. Longman, 1998

*Ross, Stewart. *Arab-Israeli Conflict*. Steck-Vaughn Company, 1996

Schulzinger, Robert D. *A Time For War— The United States and Vietnam, 1941–1975*. Oxford University Press Inc., 1997

*Townshend, Charles (editor). *The Oxford Illustrated History of Modern Warfare*. Oxford University Press Inc., 1997

*Wright, David. *Vietnam War*. Steck-Vaughn Company, 1996

Young, John W. *Cold War Europe, 1945–1991—A Political History*. St. Martin's Press Inc., 1996

INDEX

ACKNOWLEDGMENTS

Cover (main picture) TRH Pictures/U.S. Army, (inset) TRH Pictures/United Nations; page 1 Robert Hunt Library; page 5 Robert Hunt Library; page 7 Robert Hunt Library; page 9 TRH Pictures; page 10 TRH Pictures; page 13 TRH Pictures; page 14 TRH Pictures/United States Marine Corps; page 17 TRH Pictures; page 18 Robert Hunt Library; page 19 Robert Hunt Library; page 20 Robert Hunt Library; page 22 Robert Hunt Library; page 23 TRH Pictures/Imperial War Museum; page 24 Robert Hunt Library; page 26 Robert Hunt Library; page 27 Robert Hunt Library; page 29 Robert Hunt Library; page 30 Robert Hunt Library; page 32 TRH Pictures/Imperial War Museum; page 34 TRH Pictures; page 37 TRH Pictures/United Nations; page 38 Robert Hunt Library; page 39 Robert Hunt Library; page 40 TRH Pictures/U.S. Department of Defense; page 42 TRH Pictures/United States Air Force; page 46 Robert Hunt Library; page 48 TRH Pictures; page 49 TRH Pictures/U.S. Department of Defense; page 50 Robert Hunt Library; page 51 TRH Pictures; page 53 TRH Pictures/Pacemaker; page 54 TRH Pictures; page 55 TRH Pictures; page 56 Rex Features Ltd.; page 57 Rex Features Ltd.; page 58 TRH Pictures; page 60 Robert Hunt Library; page 62 TRH Pictures/U.S. Army; page 64 TRH Pictures/U.S. Army; page 65 TRH Pictures/U.S. Army; page 66 TRH Pictures/U.S. Army; page 67 TRH Pictures; page 68 TRH Pictures; page 72 TRH Pictures/United States Air Force; page 73 TRH Pictures/U.S. Navy; page 74 TRH Pictures; page 75 TRH Pictures/United Nations; page 76 TRH Pictures/J.-P. Husson; page 77 TRH Pictures/United States Air Force.